PLAN FOR YOUR LIFE

How to Live a Healthy and Safe Lifestyle
From Two Expert Insurance Agents

BY GREG BOYD
WITH JASON GRAYBEAL

Edited by Hilary Jastram, www.jhilcreative.com

RESOURCES

GraybealGroup.com

Greg@GraybealGroup.com

Facebook.com/GregBoyd3rd

Facebook.com/GraybealGroup

LinkedIn.com/in/Greg-Boyd-GraybealGroup

Instagram.com/GregBoyd3rd

TABLE OF CONTENTS

INTRODUCTION

We live in an age of rapid change and deepening uncertainty. Perhaps more than ever before in our lifetimes, we have no idea what tomorrow will bring. But one thing we do know is how much we want to protect those things that are precious to us—our family and friends, our homes and other property, and our well-being. That, at least, is a constant in our busy lives.

We also know that, despite these unchanging needs, we face challenges and risks to them that call for sensible preparation and timely action. The aim of this book is to give you the information and tools you can use to meet those challenges. By knowing how to cut the risks and how to respond effectively in an accident or crisis, you can substantially improve your security and the welfare of those who matter so much to you as you gain some peace of mind.

Oftentimes, safekeeping is a matter of commonsense. But in the hectic whirl of life or the heat of the moment, commonsense can fly out of the window, and we end up making decisions that may not turn out to be for the best. That is why it pays to think ahead—to take precautions before trouble confronts you and to gain the knowledge that will help you keep a level head if it turns up.

Above all, it seems to me, after considerable experience of helping others do just that; there are five vital things that you need to do to protect yourself and your precious ones most effectively.

Make the time to review and understand the risks that surround you. Don't put it off to another day. It needn't take long, and you can do some of it from the comfort of your favorite armchair with pen and paper.

Take the appropriate action to minimize those risks. Often, this does not need to cost much, or indeed, anything.

Be prepared to deal with a crisis in a calm and intelligent manner. You can do this if you already know what you will do if an emergency does arise.

Let others—your kids, your partner, your employees, or work colleagues —know how important these things are, what you've done to protect them, and what they should do to protect themselves.

Insure yourself against the threats to the safekeeping of your family, your prosperity, and your property.

This book can help you do that. I don't claim that it has all the answers, but I have a lifetime of experience in dealing with many of the issues covered here. So often, I encounter people whose guiding principle seems to be: "It won't happen to me." Then it did.

Now here's the good news. This isn't a gloomy book. From time to time, it might even make you smile—and that has to be good. It is packed with easy-to-understand information that can help improve your life, from security and accident prevention to personal health—covering issues like diet, nutrition, exercise, and medications—and key insurance topics. It pinpoints the danger spots in your home, highlights special safety needs for vulnerable people like children and seniors, provides advice on how to plan for and cope with emergency incidents big and small, and explains what you need to know about food safety. It also provides guidance on workplace safety, spotlights the dangers on our roads and highways, helps you stay safe on vacation, and alerts you to the main scam tricks that con artists might try to pull on you.

My role in providing solutions does not, of course, end there. The final chapter focuses on the key issue of insurance. Again, the intention is to provide an overview of some of the most important types of insurance and offer some initial guidance on how to establish the types and coverage you need. The fact is that, without insurance, you cannot minimize the impact of the risks every one of us—from a newborn baby to the president of the United States—faces.

These days, the insurance business is increasingly complex and intensely competitive. It's easy to go online and shop around for a policy but, unless you're an expert, the chance of finding exactly what you need at the right price is quite remote. All too often, people find themselves "comparing apples with oranges" and making decisions based simply on cost, only to discover in their time of need that they don't have the coverage they thought they did.

The internet is a fantastic source of information and, as I have said, you can discover a lot more about safety and health issues right there on your PC. But who is there to discuss your very specific needs, to provide customized policies that precisely fit in with your individual requirements and your budget, to know exactly who offers the best policy and rates, and to advise you on how to adjust your coverage as your needs change?

Your knowledgeable insurance agents are here for you to do just that. Your well-being and your protection are our concerns ... as you will see in this book.

CHAPTER ONE

PROTECTING ALL THAT SURROUNDS YOU

I don't know about you, but every time I look around my home or walk into someone else's, I mentally cringe and think, *could be better*. It's not the furnishings, decorations, or cleanliness that bothers me. It's the safety hazards and security risks. Once you tune into this stuff, you spot the flaws in every corner.

The trouble is, we're all so busy leading our supercharged lives that either we don't notice the warning signs or we just don't do anything about them. Or we push them back on the honey-do list with a mental "I'll get around to it" note.

But we never do.

Where to start in making your home a safer place to live?

Well, the first thing is to avoid getting overwhelmed by the task. You can't do it all at once. You have to work out your priorities. That may depend on where you live, who lives with you, and what's already been done to protect you.

For instance, if you live in a low-crime area and have a young family, maybe kid-proofing your home will go ahead of installing a burglar alarm. Or, if you have older or disabled folk in your household, solving their needs may be top of the list.

Spend a little while thinking this through, weighing what needs to be done against your available time and budget. You may decide to do things in a different order than the way I present them here. But whatever you do, first take a walk around your house, inside and out, and jot down some notes about what needs to be done under the following headings:

Security – What do you need to do to make your home safe from intruders? What are the most vulnerable places? Doors? Windows? Basements?

Fire and Fume Hazards – Are there, particularly risky places? Are there smokers (both human and stoves) in the house? Where's the ventilation? What about the clothes dryer vent?

Possible Accident Spots – Such as floor coverings, staircases, clutter (like in a teen's bedroom!), doors that open the "wrong" way, and loose or worn fittings.

Storage – From medications and laundry supplies, through weapons, to emergency supplies like flashlights. How safe are they? How accessible?

Safety and Switch-Off Points – Check locations and accessibility of alarms and utility shut-offs. Do you know where they are and how to enable/disable them? Are they fully functional?

Get the picture? You'll learn a lot more about these safety areas in the next few pages – and how to make them safe.

Let's get started.

HOW TO PROTECT YOUR HOME AND SAVE MONEY

As far as I'm concerned, home safety boils down to two things—protecting your home and possessions and taking care of yourself and your family. Let's start with the building and contents.

THINGS THAT WON'T COST YOU A CENT

You don't have to turn your home into a fortress or spend a lot of money to make your place a heck-of-a-lot tougher for thieves to penetrate. In fact, there are a few things you can do that won't cost a cent. I'm thinking here about keeping your doors and windows locked whenever possible, the garage door shut, letting trustworthy neighbors know and canceling newspaper and mail deliveries when you're going away and fixing those shaky old fences.

Don't hide an emergency door key outside—thieves know all the "secret" places you believe they'll never think of, including that little bunny-rabbit figurine with the hidden compartment underneath. And be wary about trusting a youngster with an entry key. Give it to a relative or neighbor. Don't even keep your main key with items that identify your address, and never leave it in your car.

While we're on the subject of cars, you do always close your windows (leaving breathing space for pets if you have them) and lock the doors when you leave it, don't you? Of course, you never leave your engine running while you dash across to the ATM?

LOW-BUDGET ROUTE TO PEACE OF MIND

Here's a comforting thought. When you spend just a small amount of money to improve your home security, you substantially reduce the risk of being burglarized. Even better, you may be able to cut your insurance premium—different insurers have different rules, so you'll need to investigate this.

You can buy a window lock for less than a dollar, a door safety chain for a couple of bucks, and a peephole that lets you view visitors before opening the door for just a little more. They're all simple to install but, if it's beyond your ability, find a friend, neighbor, or relative who can help.

If your door locks and latches are old, or if you lost a key, replace them, making sure the new ones have a deadbolt at least one inch long. If your door has glass that a thief could break to reach through to the handle inside, consider a double deadbolt that has a key lock on each side—BUT always leave the key in the inside lock when you're at home otherwise you won't be able to escape in an emergency.

Beyond this, we're talking home security alarms and detectors, but again it doesn't need to cost you a fortune. As I write this, I just did a quick check online and found systems at one big internet retailer starting from as little as $25. It was wireless too—easy to install, with no messy wiring to do.

However, I'm not necessarily saying this is the way to go. It depends on your neighborhood crime risk, your personal vulnerability (for instance, if you live alone), and your budget. You generally get what you pay for, and this is an area where you might want to consult a professional—both about your needs and to do the installation. But if you do this, make sure you get two or, preferably, three competitive bids.

More sophisticated systems might include external audible alarms, external lighting directed at your home, cameras, internal motion sensors, and even direct links to the security company that alerts them if your home is broken into. You can get more information on these options, including local experts from the National Burglar & Fire Alarm Association, at alarm.org.

WATCH OUT FOR SMOOTH TALKERS

You can have all the security systems in the world in place, but they're of limited value if you let a burglar in through your front door. These characters come in all sorts of guises—like phony utility workers or someone asking for a glass of water or to use your bathroom or phone—but they all have a convincing story to tell.

They may even distract you inside or outside your home while an accomplice gets to work or open a door or window so they can return later. The solution is not to let anyone into your house (nor go outside with them) unless you're 110% sure of who they are. Check their credentials and, if necessary, phone their supposed employers before letting them in.

PROTECT YOURSELF FROM FIRE AND FUMES

Wouldn't it be just great if we could build totally fireproof homes? I mean, building materials, furnishings, and clothing that just didn't burn. Technically, I suppose it's possible, but it'd cost you a small fortune. Since most of us can't go that route, let me tell you about the four things I've done in my home—bearing in mind that the most important thing in any home fire is the safety and survival of the occupants.

1. Installed fire/smoke alarms (a few dollars each) in all main rooms and hallways, and I check the batteries regularly. If you already have them and they're more than 10 years old, I recommend you replace them.

2. Bought a fire escape ladder that I keep on an easily-accessible shelf on the landing in case fire traps anyone upstairs. If you buy one, make sure everyone knows how to use it!

3. Placed a fire extinguisher in an entryway closet. This only works if you take the time to learn how to use it (and what sort of fires it works on), regularly replace it, and use it only to tackle small fires— and then only AFTER calling 911.

4. Developed a simple fire safety and escape plan that I discussed with my family. The number one rule: Get out of the house and stay out. My plan included talking to my kids about fire dangers and appropriate behavior.

By the way, you may find that your local fire department offers free home checks and even free or cheap alarms.

You should also install at least one carbon monoxide alarm in your home (preferably near the bedrooms), which will pick up on fumes from furnaces, fires, and other appliances and vehicles that reach a dangerous level in your home.

WEATHER-PROOFING YOUR HOME

Would-be burglars and wayward flames are the most obvious threats to the security of your home. But there are others. Take the weather, for instance. It never ceases to surprise us—or the meteorologists!

But there are a few simple steps you can take to minimize weather impact on your home and family. Lagging exposed pipes are probably the first thing that comes to mind—and I don't mean just outside either. One home a client owned was plumbed for laundry appliances in the garage. They never used the system but completely overlooked the fact that it was still full of water—until the thaw after a particularly cold spell!

On the other hand, when the weather is hot and dry, it's your body more than your home that you have to think about—in terms of keeping well-hydrated and staying cool. Don't forget to take care of the maintenance of your air conditioning and ventilation systems and to follow any advisories on brush clearance in a fire-risk area.

If you live in a storm, tornado, flood, or hurricane-prone area, your basic safety rules include monitoring weather warnings, securing all vulnerable areas, including doors and windows, and knowing what to do if the worst happens.

SAFES – EVERY HOME SHOULD HAVE ONE

A good safe is your final line of defense if someone does break into your home or if fire threatens to destroy valuables and important documents. In my opinion, every home should have one, and it should be bolted to the floor, preferably a concrete floor or a joist.

It makes sense to keep really important stuff that you don't regularly need in a bank safety deposit box but, for jewelry you wear frequently or documents you consult regularly, a small fireproof safe will meet your needs.

It should go without saying that if you keep weapons or other potentially dangerous items at home, they should always be under lock and key.

KEEPING YOUR FAMILY HEALTHY & SAFE AT HOME

Watch out for that wet floor. Whoops! Too late. Mind that you don't bang your head. *Ouch!* "Don't eat that." *Oh no!* I guess we've all been there, done that, and we have the scars to prove it! You let your guard down for a minute, and disaster walks through the door.

There's just no way you can guarantee total safety in a home. But there's a whole lot you can do to eliminate the vast majority of risks. Did you spot anything on that home and yard tour I advised a few pages back? I'd be surprised if you didn't. Most of our problems are down to carelessness and thoughtlessness, and there are a few basic rules I can give you right now about dealing with them.

BASIC HOME SAFETY TIPS THAT COULD SAVE A LIFE

Falls are the most common cause of accidents in the home, a substantial proportion of them serious or even fatal. You can cut the risk of these and maybe save a life by:

1. Ensuring carpets are properly fixed to the floor (use floor-gripper tape for loose rugs on slippery surfaces, and ensure fitted carpets are fastened down).

2. Removing clutter, especially in busy "traffic" areas.

3. Marking temporary hazards—like a ladder that people don't expect to encounter—with a piece of brightly colored cloth and removing it as soon as you're done.

4. Keeping floors dry or out of bounds when wet. You can buy specialty absorbent rugs for particularly dangerous areas like the kitchen, laundry, and bathroom.

5. Installing handrails in bathrooms or wherever there are steps (including the yard). This is especially important if you have older folk living with or visiting you.

6. Repairing and leveling walkways in the yard.

7. Installing low-wattage lighting along driveways and paths that are used at night.

Fires and fumes, which I talked about a few pages back, are another key area of home safety. In addition to the measures I recommended then, it's also important to make sure all rooms are properly ventilated, heating appliances are inspected and serviced annually, air ducts and filters are regularly cleaned, and lint filters on clothes dryers are cleared out after each use. Blocked lint filters and dryer vents are a major cause of fumes and fires.

Finally, I want to warn about keeping dangerous stuff out of reach. I'm talking not only about your medications, including prescription and over-the-counter stuff but about weapons, as well. There are also other dangers you may not immediately recognize, like poisonous house plants, cleaning products, and cosmetics, and heavy or fragile objects that could cause mayhem if they fall or are broken.

This is especially important if you have young people or pets around your home. You can get a list of poisons from both the American Association of Poison Control Centers and the ASPCA Animal Poison Control Center.

CHILDPROOF AND PET-PROOF YOUR HOME

I was visiting some elderly friends of mine a while back and noticed how many power outlets were uncovered at ground level. They were proudly showing me pictures of their year-old great-grandson and were excited because the youngster and his parents would be visiting the following weekend.

"You know," I said, "he's going to be crawling around everywhere. You need to get those outlets covered. While you're at it, make sure he can't get to them and pull out the plugs that are connected. And maybe you need a plan for how you're going to stop him crawling up your stairs."

The point is you don't need to be an active parent to need to childproof your home. In fact, many of the same measures you'd take to keep kids safe in your house or apartment also apply to pets.

I already mentioned keeping poisons, weapons, and ornaments out of reach. But there are plenty of other things you should do to protect little ones and furry friends. If you're on the internet, you can download a guide but here, in summary, is the list:

1. Safety locks and catches on cabinets and drawers wherever they're accessible.

2. Safety gates across doorways and stairs.

3. Doorknob covers and door locks to prevent access to out-of-bounds rooms.

4. Anti-scald devices on faucets and showerheads.

5. Smoke alarms.

6. Window guards and safety netting to help prevent falls from windows, balconies, decks, and landings.

7. Corner and edge bumpers to cushion sharp edges on furniture and fireplaces.

8. Outlet covers and outlet plates (as I told my senior friends).

9. Carbon monoxide alarm.

10. A tassel on each separate window blind cord and inner miniblind cord-stops to prevent strangulation.

11. Anchors to avoid furniture and appliance tip-overs.

12. Layers of protection around pools and spas—a barrier completely surrounding the area, including a 4-foot-tall fence and a self-closing, self-latching gate.

When I had a young family, I also made a point to educate my older kids about re-securing or removing any potentially dangerous items or gateways after they used them.

Don't forget the basic child safety rules about never leaving them unattended in or near any water, whether it's the tub or a pool (even a paddling pool).

This is by no means an exhaustive list either. You can get lots more information online. The independent Consumer Reports organization also publishes its own *Guide to Childproofing & Safety*. You can buy or order it online or at a bookstore.

TAKING CARE OF OUR SENIOR CITIZENS

These days, many seniors seem as young in mind and body as younger folk. They work hard at staying that way.

But this can make it easy to overlook the vulnerability of the less able—like the couple I was talking about earlier, one of whom suffers badly from arthritis and the other who can be (like many of us at times!) very forgetful.

When it comes to their personal safety, the key issues are fall-prevention, and remembering to take medications, which can be solved by using a multi-compartment storage container labeled with the names of each day and refilled at the end of the week.

I also advised my friends to think about subscribing to a home alert system. One of them can wear an alarm linked to a care-alert service if they are home alone. If something goes wrong, and they are unable to get to the phone, they can still get help. They did this, and I know it brought them great peace of mind.

Whether we're seniors or not, we all have a duty to keep an eye out for those who are more vulnerable than ourselves, checking on them when we see them—and when we don't.

HYGIENE FOR HEALTH

A great thing about meeting people from other cultures is to share in some of their wisdom. One of my clients is Lebanese. He always looks so smartly dressed whenever we meet and, come to think of it, I've never known him to be sick in the 20-some years we've been acquainted.

I mentioned this to him one time, and he quoted back to me what he said was a well-known Lebanese proverb: "Hygiene is two-thirds of health." Amen to that. If I'm putting your home and personal hygiene under the microscope, will I like what I see? That depends on how seriously you take the subject!

Although personal cleanliness is absolutely essential to your well-being, there are, in fact, just two basic rules that account for most of your hygiene-related health and that of others you live with. It all boils down to regularly washing your hands and covering your mouth and nose when you cough or sneeze.

Dirty hands and uncovered noses are undoubtedly the main transmitters of germs and viruses in the home. You should always wash your hands in hot, soapy water after a bathroom visit, before handling food, before and after cleaning up a young child, and after you've been out— whether it's a trip to the grocery store or a gardening session in the yard.

There's quite an art to washing your hands properly. The Centers for Disease Control offers very useful guidance on their website. Just search for "handwashing."

If you cough or sneeze into your hands, you need to wash them directly after. But always carry a handkerchief or facial tissues with you anyway. Please don't sneeze onto your sleeve!

These simple rules are important to pass on to youngsters, who always seem to forget the basics like brushing their teeth. Which reminds me, oral hygiene—brushing, rinsing, and flossing—is as important to me as keeping my hands clean.

It's not just for the benefit of those within "breath range" but also because the human mouth is where all the food bacteria and germs meet daily for a party!

The other side of the hygiene story lurks in your bathroom and kitchen. Keeping a clean bathroom is easy, with bleach and other household cleaning products (remember my earlier advice about storing them out of reach). The more that room is used, the more you use them.

The kitchen is a different story. All sorts of creatures, masquerading under the posh title of "micro-organisms," lurk on counter-tops and dishes, in the dishwasher, toaster, stove, and refrigerator, and just about anywhere else where food has been.

The problem is that you can't just splash toxic cleaning products about where they might come into contact with food, although there are a number of products on the market that can kill bacteria without harming you.

Let me run through my own checklist of kitchen hygiene tips to help you out here. Again, it's not exhaustive, but it will cover you in the case of most dangers.

- ❑ When you're preparing food, if you have long hair, tie it back or cover it. Remove jewelry.

- ❑ Wash and thoroughly rinse your hands before doing any kitchen work (including cooking); dry them on a paper towel.

- ❑ Clean all cooking utensils and work surfaces with an antibacterial agent (read the instructions) before and after using them. If you wash and dry dishes by hand, leave them in a drying rack rather than wiping them with a tea towel.

- ❑ Use several cutting boards, and make sure to scrub and use hot water on them after you're done. Use a separate board for meat. Plastic boards can go in the dishwasher and should be regularly replaced.

- ❑ Know and apply the minimum temperatures for cooking foods.

- ❑ The same goes for refrigerator, freezer, and open-air storage times of different foods. Store meat and vegetables separately. Return unused food to the fridge or freezer as quickly as possible.

❑ Always wash fruit and vegetables before preparing or cooking them.

❑ If you use a spoon or fork to taste food as you cook, don't use it again until it's been thoroughly cleaned. Use another one instead.

❑ Hot-wash and frequently replace scrubbing brushes and sponges.

❑ Food: If it doesn't look or smell right, then it probably isn't. Toss it!

❑ One final thing. Please keep kids and animals out of the kitchen. They're at risk when present, and so is your kitchen hygiene. Finally, don't wash pet dishes along with your own stuff!

INSURING HOUSE AND HEALTH RISKS

As I said at the outset, there's no way you can avoid every possible safety and health risk that crops up in your home. That's why we have insurance. It's an absolutely essential part of living a healthy and safe lifestyle.

In the final chapter of this book, I'll be talking in more detail about how best to cover your insurance needs in the key risk areas. Let me just say for now that if you have an insurance-related question as to the points I've outlined, please don't hesitate to contact our office.

CHAPTER TWO

YOUR ACTION PLAN WHEN THINGS GO WRONG

DON'T PANIC!

That's the first and most critical piece of advice to follow when trouble shows up in your home. Sure, that's easier said than done, but when you're in a tight corner unless it's a life-or-death moment, allow yourself five or 10 seconds to take a deep breath and mentally tell yourself not to panic. It may seem like you're burning up precious time but, believe me, you'll likely waste even more if you don't do that.

What you do next depends on the nature of the incident.

ACCIDENTS AND FIRST AID

You'd probably be a unique person if you got through a lifetime without experiencing or encountering an accident that causes injury, either at home or in the workplace. My own collection includes being dropped on my head during a "fireman's carry" experiment conducted by my older brother, piercing my foot with a garden fork, and fainting after jumping up quickly from a crouching position after introducing a hammer-head to my thumb while building a rabbit hutch. And then, there's the rest of the family …

Your first decision is whether the incident calls for hospitalization or other medical attention. Loss of consciousness, heavy blood loss or vomiting of blood, inability to move all or part of the body (by the individual, not you, unless you're the victim), severe burns, damage to the eyes, head injuries (like the one I suffered) and breathing difficulties, all suggest a medical emergency and to call 911.

Never try to move someone injured in a fall, although there may be other things you can do to provide temporary relief.

If the individual is able to move himself or herself without pain, you might be able to take them to the ER if traffic congestion is not likely to be a problem on the way, but, if in doubt, wait for the paramedics.

Bottom line: If you're not sure, call 911.

If it's not that kind of an emergency, or if you can take action before professional help arrives, here are some quick, basic guidelines on what you could do for the following incidents:

1. **Burns**

   For minor burns, soak the affected area in cool (not iced) water for five to 10 minutes, then apply a soothing cream like aloe vera or antibiotic ointment (don't use oil or butter). Cover with a dry dressing. Seek medical help for more severe burns, and don't try to remove any clothing stuck to the burnt skin.

2. **Bites and Stings**

   If stung, remove the stinger if you can. Apply an icepack to reduce swelling, followed by hydrocortisone cream, and take an antihistamine pill (both of which you can buy over the counter). Severe reactions like breathing difficulty or swelling of the lips and throat could indicate allergic or other problems, and you should call 911. CPR may be necessary. You should also always seek medical advice about bites from animals or poisonous insects, or even a severe scratch from a cat.

3. Choking

Choking is usually an emergency, and you should call 911. In desperate circumstances, if someone is choking on food, for example, you might be able to clear the airway by performing an abdominal thrust. Ideally, you should learn this through First Aid training.

4. Cuts and Scratches

Clean the wound with cool, running water. Using stronger liquids, like alcohol, can make things worse. Apply pressure with a cloth to try to stop bleeding. Moderate bleeding is okay—it helps the cleaning process. But get medical help if the cut is deep and/or it doesn't slow after a few minutes or if there's something lodged inside the wound. Leaving a minor wound uncovered (but clean) will help it heal more quickly.

5. Food Poisoning

Most food poisoning is mild and will subside in a day or two. Avoid solids, drink frequent sips of clear liquids, and resume eating with small amounts of low-fat foods. Seek medical advice if the person is a child, can't hold liquids down, or if symptoms are severe or persist for more than three days.

6. Nosebleeds

Nosebleeds are common and usually not serious. They may be more likely with certain medications or allergies. To stop the bleeding, pinch the front of the nostrils and push toward the face, with the head leaning slightly forward. Hold this position for five minutes. You can also apply an ice pack to the nose or cheeks. If the bleeding can't be stopped and is exceptionally heavy, or the person is dizzy or faint, seek medical help.

7. Sunburn and Heatstroke

These are totally different afflictions, although they spring from the same source—the sun. When it comes to treating both, get out of the sun and into a cool place. Apply aloe vera or other lotion to ease sunburn; drink plenty of cool water (not caffeinated sodas) and take a cool bath to reduce the effects of heatstroke. If symptoms like dizziness and nausea persist, see a doctor.

8. Tetanus

If the victim suffers a skin-breaking wound, the person may need a tetanus shot to prevent infection. Tetanus is a severe bacterial infection that hits muscles and nerves, but often, you're not aware of it until a week or two after an injury. It's preventable through immunization every 10 years. So if it's been more than 10 years since you had a shot, get one, especially after an injury with an open wound.

DEALING WITH SUDDEN, SEVERE ILLNESS

Heart attacks, strokes, loss of consciousness, and high fevers demand immediate medical attention. Very often, the faster you can get treatment, the more likely the patient is to survive and recover. Time is of the essence!

In these cases, being able to spot the early warning signs could be critical. Chest tightness or pain, especially radiating to the left arm, and breathing problems could signal a heart condition, while numbness in various parts of the body, confusion, vision or speech problems, dizziness, balance difficulties, and inexplicable, severe headaches may indicate the onset of a stroke.

For more about these symptoms and how to respond, check out AmericanHeart.org and StrokeAssociation.org.

As for fevers, anything around 100 degrees in a child and a sustained temperature of 103 degrees and over in an adult should get you to a doctor. (This is only a guideline; even earlier action may be necessary if there are other worrying symptoms, such as chronic sleepiness in a child.)

I've noticed a lot of debate in the media recently about CPR (cardio-pulmonary resuscitation) techniques. In the past, First responders used to recommend mouth-to-mouth resuscitation, but now some (though not all) say the best thing to do is pump the victim's chest forcefully, at up to 100 compressions a minute. The jury's out on this, but it seems likely that compressions are key because they also force air out of the lungs at the same time.

If you run your own business, you may want to consider having a portable, automatic defibrillator. If you do this, ensure you have someone who knows how to use it!

IMPROVING YOUR FIRST AID SKILLS

If you're not a First-Aider or you don't have one in your immediate family or small business, take my advice: Get to it! If you'll pardon the pun, I've only just scratched the surface with the guidance outlined here. These days, there's no shortage of information and help, from books that cost just a few dollars (for example, the American Medical Association's *Handbook of First Aid and Emergency Care* costs about $15) to intensive courses run by commercial organizations and the American Red Cross.

You can study (and gain certifications) online, but in my opinion, there's no substitute for attending classes, where you can ask questions, watch others, and focus on particular areas where you need skills or have concerns. Because it's an independent, non-profit, charitable organization, the Red Cross is a good place to start. Visit redcross.org and key in your zip code or find them in the phone book for details on local training.

KEY INGREDIENTS FOR YOUR FIRST AID KIT

Piggybacking on my advice in the previous section, if you don't have a first aid kit, please get one. Today, if you can. It could save a life. Plus, they're not expensive and, if you do it yourself, they're easy to put together. These days, though, you can buy ready-made kits. Drugstores and online retailers sell them, but you can also buy them from your local American Red Cross Chapter, or the Red Cross Store online. Costs range from around $15 to $50. The Red Cross also provides guidance on what you should have in a good First Aid kit.

In a business, you will need something more substantial, depending on the number of employees and type of work being done. There may also be state and national legal requirements as to what you are required to have on hand.

WHAT TO DO IF YOU'RE A VICTIM OF A CRIME

I hope this doesn't happen to you. But it happens to millions of Americans every year: They're on the receiving end of a criminal activity.

What you do depends on the nature and severity of the crime, who is involved, and the stage of the crime. Regardless, there are certain firm rules you should follow.

WHEN A CRIME IS IN PROGRESS

The safety and security of children and other vulnerable individuals come first. Take whatever steps you can to move them to safety, then try to put a barrier between yourself and the criminal—getting out of a house or locking yourself on a roof, for instance.

If you are accosted by a thief, at home or in the street, give them whatever they ask for. Don't argue, fight, or try to conceal items. If you suspect someone is in your house or on your property, call 911—who, by the way, would never recommend that you tackle an intruder who could be armed or physically powerful.

If you suspect you are being stalked, contact the police. If you're threatened with a street attack, try to run away if you can, making as much noise as possible. If you are being forcibly held, your voice, your elbows, and your knees are your strongest defenses.

AFTER A CRIME HAS BEEN COMMITTED

Here is a basic checklist of the things you should do (depending on the nature of the crime):

- ❑ Ensure everyone is out of danger.

- ❑ Check the well-being of anyone else who was involved.

- ❑ Call 911.

- ❑ Administer First Aid, if required.

- ❑ Identify witnesses, if appropriate

- ❑ After a theft or burglary, try not to touch anything at the scene until the police arrive.

- ❑ Re-secure your property.

- ❑ Make an inventory of what has been damaged or stolen.

- ❑ If you are a victim of crime abroad, contact the US Embassy or consulate in the host location, as well as the local police.

- ❑ Contact your insurer or agent and follow instructions for making a claim.

There are numerous other things that might be appropriate, depending on the advice of the police and your insurer. They are there to help and advise you, so try to follow their guidance.

LOST OR STOLEN WALLETS AND PURSES

It's bad enough to lose your precious possessions, either by accident or in a theft. But when you lose confidential items like credit cards, keys, and other personal documents, you also run the risk of becoming the victim of a further crime.

Whoever has these items might use them to steal further from you. They might take your money, items from your home or car, and even your identity.

You can minimize the risk of this happening by taking prompt action. Contact the police, of course. Then you must notify the issuers of all missing credit and debit cards, checkbooks, and traveler's checks.

This task is considerably easier if you have a separate list of issuers and banks (not in your wallet!) or the emergency numbers for them. You'll find them on your cards and other documents, or you can subscribe to a card security service that you contact via a single number, and they will look after the rest.

These cards and other documents will normally be canceled straightaway. The notification process also usually (but not always) covers you against subsequent fraudulent use of the items—so speed really is essential.

You then need to contact the issuers of any other items (like Social Security, health insurers, your state department of motor vehicles, and even your library) so that your cards are not fraudulently used and to let your insurer know.

New cards can be issued, and replacement checks can be provided quickly, although replacement Social Security cards generally are not issued.

It's possible you may become the victim of identity theft. In that case, notify the credit reporting agencies and get a fraud alert placed on your records.

Unfortunately, if the theft/loss also includes car and/or house keys, you must replace these locks as quickly as possible. Replacing car locks can be expensive and nearly as troublesome as losing your car.

Finally, it's important to keep a written note as a checklist of all the actions you have taken.

DISASTER PLANNING AND ACTION

Having a First Aid kit and undergoing training is a sound starting point in preparing to handle a disaster. By "disaster," I mean a fire, a building collapse, air contamination, or any one of the natural catastrophes that can strike certain parts of the country, like an earthquake, tornado, hurricanes, landslides, and floods. These can wreak havoc with our lives and property.

Undoubtedly, the most important things are, first, to have an effective plan of action for what you will do if any of these incidents happen, and, second, to have the equipment and supplies you might need to help you cope. For instance, as I mentioned earlier, I keep a foldable fire escape ladder upstairs in case a blaze traps anyone on my second floor.

WHAT TO DO IN A FIRE

Fires are one of the most common causes of unintentional injuries and deaths in the home, so please make sure you follow the guidance I gave earlier on installing alarms. In addition, the Federal Government offers the following tips on other things you can do to prepare for and deal with a fire at home:

- Make and practice a fire escape plan.
- Plan for two ways to escape from each room.
- Plan for everyone in your home, including babies and others who need help to escape.
- Pick a place to meet after you escape to check that everyone got out.
- Practice your escape plan every month.
- Practice getting out with your eyes closed, crawling low to the floor.
- Involve children in making and practicing your escape plan.
- Teach children to never hide during a fire. They must get out and stay out.
- Clear toys, boxes, and other debris from exits.
- Check that windows open easily. Fix any that stick.
- Be sure that security bars on doors and windows have a quick-release latch, and everyone knows how to open them.
- Never open a door that feels hot. Escape another way.
- Escape first, and then call for help.

If some of these measures sound a bit dramatic, remember that a small flame can become a big fire in less than a minute, and a home will very quickly fill with thick smoke soon afterward. That last bullet point is critical. Not only should you get out fast, but you also should never go back into a burning home. If someone is missing, tell firefighters.

I mentioned fire extinguishers earlier, but you need to be wary about their use. If they are used on the wrong type of blaze, they could make things worse. If used when the fire is already out of control, they could waste precious time and cost lives. The US Fire Administration (USFA) recommends using them only if you're trained to do so.

Many of the tips I have outlined above also apply to businesses. Having a written plan and conducting regular practices are essential. You may also have special requirements if you handle or store hazardous materials. Speak to your local fire department and invite them to do an inspection and provide guidance.

DEALING WITH OTHER CATASTROPHES

You need an action plan for other disasters that could strike your home or business. What goes into it depends on the sort of incidents that might affect you, meaning you must establish exactly what the likely risks are for your home locale.

Some measures you can take apply to most large-scale emergency situations, like taking whatever advanced steps you can to disaster-proof your building, maintaining a stock of food, water, and medical supplies in case you are isolated for any length of time, and having equipment such as flashlights and cell phones at hand.

Let's take a look at specific incidents:

1. **Earthquakes**

   Do you live or work in what the experts call a seismically active area, aka, one prone to quakes? If you don't know, or you're not sure of the risk level, check with the US Geological Survey (USGS), which provides maps showing the most vulnerable areas. If you do, here are some advance actions to consider:

   • If you're constructing or remodeling your home or business, discuss strengthening it with your contractor.

   • Secure potential hazards, like loose shelving and items needing repair.

- Have a plan that identifies safe areas, for example, under strong tables or clear areas outdoors, and ensure you know how you will communicate it with others. Make sure everyone involved knows about it.

- Store emergency equipment and supplies in an easily accessible place

- If you're unfortunate enough to suffer a quake, follow Federal Emergency Management Agency (FEMA) advice:

- If you're indoors, drop to the ground, take cover, and hold on. Outdoors, stay there, and move away from buildings, streetlights, and utility services. In a vehicle, stop as soon as you safely can and stay inside. If you're trapped, cover your mouth, and try not to move. Tap on a pipe or wall so rescuers can locate you.

By the way, even the experts can't tell you when there's going to be an earthquake, so don't believe some of those phony emails that circulate warning of an imminent quake. Just always be prepared!

2. **Floods**

The National Weather Service provides an updated map that shows the flood risk in your area and provides updates on river levels and rainfall forecasts, while FEMA gives state-by-state guidance to identify flood-prone areas. FEMA also advises that to prepare for a flood, you should:

- Avoid building in a flood-prone area unless you can raise the structure above the flood level.

- Elevate electrical equipment and panels if flooding is a risk.

- Install "check valves" in sewer traps to prevent floodwater from backing up into your drains.

- Contact community officials to find out if barriers (levees, beams, floodwalls) are planned to stop floodwater from entering the homes in your area.

- Seal basement walls to avoid seepage.

- If there's a flood alert for your area, secure your building, turn off utilities, disconnect electrical appliances and move to higher ground. If your home or workplace is already flooded, don't touch electrical equipment. Get out of the building, try to avoid walking in moving water, and use a stick to test the ground ahead.

- Sometimes, a flood might be localized—as in a pipe burst or the accidental cutting of water lines. The key action here (in addition to not touching electrical equipment) is to cut the water supply. That means you need to know where the shut-off is and how to operate it. Don't leave the task until it's too late. The valve is usually located by or near the water meter, but if you can't find it, call the water company, and ask.

3. **Storms**

Many of the tips I've listed for dealing with earthquakes and floods apply to hurricanes and tornadoes, too, especially the importance of having a plan that you share with your family or employees. Also, consider installing permanent storm shutters and roofing clips, clearing gutters and downspouts, and even building a "safe room."

During storms, tune in to local radio or TV for information, secure your home or building and, if told to do so, turn off the utilities. Evacuate if you are instructed to or if you're in a vulnerable building like a mobile home or a high-rise. If you can't evacuate and don't have a safe room, stay inside, away from windows and doors, preferably in a small interior room or closet. Again, more details are available from FEMA.

4. Wildfires

Your local fire department can advise you on the wildfire risk level for your property. Then, follow the weather and local advisories to know when the risk is high. Creating a safety zone is your key protective measure, but if your home is threatened, you should always follow evacuation guidance. If fire surrounds your property, call 911 for rescue.

ADVICE FOR VISITORS

If you're anything like me, you spend a fair amount of time visiting with friends or relatives either in your home or theirs. If the visit involves an overnight stay or more, it's a good idea to let them know about your plans or ask them about theirs.

You don't need to make a drama about this—who wants to devote a friendly conversation to the subject of disaster?! I usually introduce the issue with a "By the way...." question and a lighthearted quip before turning in, and that usually does the trick.

If your visitors or hosts have never thought of these issues, you could be doing them a favor. If they're not interested, make sure you have your own mental plan for what you'll do in an emergency.

FINALLY.....

I've mentioned the Red Cross quite a few times, but when it comes to dealing with emergencies and disasters, they know their stuff. So, check out their online presentation for information on preparing for emergencies and disasters.

I've also discussed FEMA, the Federal Emergency Management Agency. They produce a wide range of publications and guidance for dealing with all kinds of disasters, including incidents for which I simply didn't have the space to cover here—such as chemical alerts, landslides, and tsunamis—as well as provide valuable advice on recovery and rebuilding after a disaster.

Further contact details are listed at the end of the book. For businesses, guidance may also be available from OSHA.

CHAPTER THREE

STAYING SAFE IN THE BEAUTIFUL OUTDOORS

I heard a story about a flying car that landed in a Stamford, Connecticut yard. First, it went off the road, then hit a wall, went airborne, bounced off the roof of a house, and finally landed in the yard of a neighboring home. Fortunately, the driver wasn't seriously injured, and there was no one in the yard. It goes to show that you might take all the yard safety measures you can think of, but you can't plan for an auto-landing on your lawn!

Barring that, there are many things you can do to make your yard a safe haven. After all, it's supposed to be there to beautify your surroundings and provide enjoyment.

10 GOLDEN RULES OF YARD AND GARDEN SAFETY

We're going to dig a lot deeper as we go through this, but I wanted to start off with what I call my *10 Golden Rules of Yard and Garden Safety*. Memorize and use these, and you will be well on the way to protecting your family and yourself from the many dangers that lurk even within the boundaries of your own property.

1. Protect children from every water element, whether it's a shallow pond, fountain, rain or water butt, or pool.

2. Before using any product or equipment, read the instructions or manual. Don't rush this job.

3. Clear the clutter around your yard, and keep all tools and chemicals out of reach of children.

4. Have the right tools for the job, including protective gear. No loose clothing if you are using machinery.

5. Power equipment or sharp tools and people don't mix. If anyone enters your work area, STOP, and get them clear before resuming.

6. When cooking outdoors, follow food hygiene rules, operate the BBQ as the manual says, and keep kids and others away from your cooking area.

7. Wear appropriate clothing for the weather, so you don't suffer from extremes of heat and cold. Remember to cover up in sunlight.

8. Know which plants in your yard are poisonous, and protect children and pets from them.

9. Keep your First Aid kit properly stocked and easily accessible.

10. Pay special attention to the needs and safety of pets. Clean up their messes immediately.

Now let's put some of these issues under the microscope for a close-up look.

KEY SAFETY CONSIDERATIONS

KID CARE

Children often don't know about danger until they learn the hard way. They don't know about "hot" until they get burned; they may have no idea what electricity is or how machinery works; some toddlers don't know you can't breathe underwater, and they are all more curious than a cat.

Yes, you can tell them all the rules, but they're kids, and rules are there to be broken in their minds. What I want you to realize is first, children don't understand risk; second, never assume they are safe when they're out of your sight; and third, and most crucially, it's your job to protect them.

The younger they are, the greater the risks. And the more risks there are—like when you're having a yard or pool party—the tougher it is to keep them all in sight and under control. At least one adult for every three kids is a good guideline.

Water is probably the biggest danger, and the basic rule is that you should never let youngsters near it unless you're there too (and, if it's a pool, that you know how to swim and perform resuscitation). Tragically, toddlers have been known to drown in just a couple of inches of water, so adult supervision is vital at all times. Be alert to and warn kids against trying to jump or dive into the shallow end of the pool, too.

Add protection by surrounding a swimming pool with a 6-foot fence and a lockable gate and covering the pool when not in use. Your whole yard should also be securely fenced and gated, so kids can't get out, and intruders can't get in.

The same principle of keeping danger out of reach applies to your storage of garden tools and chemicals. These should be in a locked shed, toolbox, or garage and always returned immediately after use.

Don't grow poisonous plants within reach, either. Always read the information about contents and safety precautions on any chemicals you apply. Natural, organic products might be safer (but check).

Regardless of this, don't let children dig in a garden or play among plants because other dangers might lurk there. Give them a play area or a sandbox.

Finally, to repeat two of my Golden Rules: please don't use machinery and sharp tools (including the lawnmower) when children are about; and make sure they are properly protected from the sun.

PROTECTION FOR PETS

The dangers associated with water, poison plants, fencing, digging, sun exposure, and machinery mentioned above apply to pets, too. Note also that paws can be damaged by hot concrete or macadam surfaces and by lawn chemicals. Weedkillers and pest baits may also be toxic.

Watch out for rough-and-tumbles between children and pets. These can get out of hand, and even docile animals have been known to scratch or bite. Protect your children and other humans by removing pet waste promptly.

The American Society for Prevention of Cruelty to Animals is a great resource for information on protecting your pet indoors and out.

MACHINERY, TOOLS, AND EQUIPMENT

After observing the rules, I've outlined about storing tools and equipment out of reach of children and not using them when others are within range, here are some safety tips to keep you out of trouble!

1. **General Advice**

   - Wear close-fitting garments and tie back long hair (so they won't get caught in machinery); use heavy-duty gloves to withstand blades and thorns and goggles where there's a risk of objects hitting your face. Don't forget earplugs when using noisy machines, and wear strong anti-slip footwear. Never operate machinery if you have used alcohol or drugs. Think of it as a DUI, with all the dangers that implies.

   - If you use gasoline to power machines, keep it safely stored in a cool place. Electricity users should always check cables for splits before plugging in and store the cords properly wound on a coil to avoid kinks and breaks.

- If you plan to dig or work near any utility lines, check the safety issues with your utility companies. You're doing them a service, too, so they don't charge for it! Also, ideally, work with a second person who can keep a lookout for "intruders" and raise the alarm if an accident happens.

2. Ladders

- Chief causes: using the wrong ladder, failing to secure it, and using it incorrectly (for example, standing on the wrong rung or stretching too far).

- The American Ladder Institute is a rich source of information both on choosing the right ladder for a particular job and then using it correctly. In particular, they stress ensuring you always have three of your four limbs in contact with the ladder at any time.

- ALI's other basic safety rules include inspecting a ladder before using it; placing it on firm, level, and non-slippery ground; not using one in high winds or if you're feeling dizzy or tired; wearing slip-resistant shoes, and never jumping down or skipping a rung.

3. Lawnmowers

- Mowers are potentially dangerous. Before mowing, check that the lawn is clear of objects but wear goggles in case you missed anything. Check the cutting height and blade guards before starting up, and then start according to the manufacturer's instructions.

- If you need to make any further adjustments, stop the mower first, unplugging it if it's electric. If it's gas-powered and needs to be refueled, switch it off and let it cool. Also, don't mow when the light is poor, especially with an electric machine where you could easily run over a cable.

- Riding-type mowers pose additional risks. They can be unstable when driven crossways on a slope. Instead, drive up and down the slope. Remember, they are (generally) built for one person—so, no passengers!

4. **Powered Loppers, Pruners, Hedge-Trimmers, and Chainsaws**

- Inspect these devices for damage to cutting edges and safety guards before powering up and work out a plan for how you will tackle your project. This is especially important when it comes to chainsaws, which can be lethal machines.

- Never use one of these machines if the handguard is missing or loose.

- Personal stability is your most important concern. Have your feet apart and firmly on the ground (not on the rungs of a ladder—I don't recommend using one for these tasks).

- If you're cutting things above you, wear a helmet. Never operate a chainsaw above shoulder height either, or you'll become unsteady—and watch out for kickback.

- Power off when you need to make adjustments or clear stuff out of the way.

5. **Chippers and Shredders**

- Grinding up wood is a noisy business, so you'll need earplugs for these machines. Protective eyewear and strong gloves are also important. Before this and before switching on, check safety guards, blades, and the power supply.

- Ensure that the chipper hood or any other fastenable parts are secure, and never attempt to loosen or adjust the machine while it is powered up. Switch off and let it stop rotating. Absolutely never reach into the machine while it is running

- Other than this, the big danger with chippers and shredders is putting the wrong materials into them. The manual will tell you the maximum diameter of branches you can insert. Stick to this guideline as you also watch out for stones and other objects getting into the machine; they can cause serious injury if ejected at speed.

6. **Sharp Tools**

- Sharp and cutting tools, like knives, pruners, saws, and drills, for example, and sharp hardware fixtures such as screws and nails, should always be safely stored when not in use. Never put an item aside while you use another one, where it is accessible to others.

- Drills and blades should be sheathed and stored facing away from you so that the handle or blunt end is easy to grasp.

- Take extra care as you transport these tools. For preference, use a tool box, or purpose-designed tool belt. If surfaces are slippery, beware! You might fall while you're carrying tools, or they might slip from your grip when using them. If you're passing a sharp item to another person, carefully hold the sharp end, so the receiver is not endangered.

- And, as always, ensure you have the right tool for the job. Making do with the wrong item or even using a blunt one calls for extra effort and runs the risk of injury.

7. **Electrical Equipment**

- Electric power is increasingly replacing gasoline for all sorts of yard tasks, but, as I suggested in the lawnmower section, the use of cables brings an extra risk of electrocution. The main rules here are:

- Outside outlets should be properly grounded and weather-shielded.

- Outlets should also be on a circuit with a Ground Fault Circuit Interrupter (GFCI). If they are not, you can buy a portable one.*

- Use only properly grounded outdoor extension cords.

- Always know where the cable is running in relation to where you're working. Never have it in a position where it could be severed.

- Check the cord carefully before and after you use it.

- No children anywhere near tools, cords, and outlets.

- If you have any concerns, questions, or installation needs, contact a qualified electrician.

The non-profit Electrical Safety Foundation International (ESFI) produces lots of useful information, including a downloadable outdoor electricity safety checklist, which also explains about GFCIs. There are contact details to get in touch with them at the end of the book.

DEALING WITH THE SUN

We love the sunshine, but it doesn't always repay us with the same level of affection. Experts say that you only need to expose yourself to continuous, direct sunlight for as little as 15 minutes to put delicate skin in danger. The hours between 10am and 4pm and late spring and early summertime are the riskiest.

The Centers for Disease Control and Prevention (CDC) offers the following "easy option" recommendations for sun protection:

1. Use sunscreen with sun protective factor (SPF) 15 or higher, reapplying every two hours.

2. Wear clothing to protect exposed skin.

3. Wear a hat with a wide brim to shade the face, head, ears, and neck.

4. Wear sunglasses that wrap around and block as close to 100% of the rays as possible.

5. Seek shade, especially during midday hours.

BARBECUE SAFETY TIPS

What fun would summer be without the taste and aroma of a barbecue? Statistics show that more people than ever are BBQing year-round. However, it's only fair to point out that some people argue that barbecues put toxins into the environment and that grilling food at high temperatures can create a cancer risk.

1. Harvard Medical School suggests that cooking meat in small pieces, choosing leaner meat, pre-cooking in a microwave, and flipping frequently could make grilled meat safer to eat.

2. Of course, food safety begins way before you fire up the BBQ. To cut the risk of bacterial infection, the Food Safety and Inspection Service (FSIS) of the US Department of Agriculture suggests buying meat and poultry as the last thing on your grocery trip and getting it home and in the refrigerator as quickly as possible. It should then be fully thawed

before cooking but kept cold (in an insulated chest if you're traveling) until you're ready to cook.

3. In keeping with the guidance I gave earlier, clean utensils and platters thoroughly and cook food thoroughly, keeping it hot until it's served.

4. Don't put cooked meat on the same platter that held raw meat, says FSIS, and refrigerate leftovers promptly.

5. When you barbecue, you're dealing with naked flames, hot surfaces, pressurized gas, and hopefully, a whole lot of people who are enjoying themselves. But they also may not be thinking about the potential hazards close by.

6. Your home city or county may have specific regulations dealing with barbecue safety, and you should check this with your local fire department. Beyond that, here are some basic safety rules to follow:

   • The grill should be at least 10 feet from any building structures or trees on a flat non-flammable surface.

   • Follow the manufacturer's instructions in usage, checking burner and tube condition and cylinder connections before using.

   • When lighting charcoal, use only special barbecue starter fluid and then only sparingly.

   • Store spare propane canisters in a cool place (but not indoors), away from the grill. Keep children away from the grill area and never leave it unattended while lit.

   • Have water in buckets or through a garden hose for dousing close. Note that you should never use water on a grease fire.

- Never pour flammable fluids onto an open flame, and keep alcoholic drinks away from the area! You can always celebrate when you're done.

- When using propane barbecues, shut off the fuel at both the bottle and the grill when you've finished cooking.

- In case of a fire, warn everyone to clear the area and, if you can do so without risk, turn off the propane or electric supply (or close the lid on a charcoal burner). Call 911 if there's any risk to personal safety or property.

OUTDOOR SAFETY FOR SMALL BUSINESSES

Maybe your outdoors is just a small parking lot and a few shrubs, but there still are risks. Look at my Golden Rules when thinking about this and consider poisonous plants, clutter, the First Aid kit to be on hand, and the right equipment and protection for whoever looks after the space.

Lighting might be important too, especially in the winter months. Also, always ensure parking bays are properly marked, with sufficient room and visibility for driving maneuvers. If staff smoke outside, ensure you/they comply with smoking area regulations and that they have somewhere safe to extinguish their cigarettes.

FINALLY ...

Most of the rules and advice I've provided are based on common sense. But I've found that isn't always around when you need it.

Above all, I can't emphasize enough the need to think about two things in your yard: child safety and your own personal behavior with tools and other equipment.

You can insure against lots of yard risks, but you never want to be in the situation of having to make a claim—so do everything you can to protect against that.

CHAPTER FOUR

DYNAMIC DUO GUARDS
HEALTH & SAFETY AT WORK

Let's start with some good news: According to the National Safety Council, US workers are actually safer at work than they are at home or in their communities. Now the bad news: Every week, close to 100 people die in preventable workplace tragedies, and millions are injured or fall victim to a reportable sickness at work.

A sobering thought, isn't it? And the cost is astronomical. If you're in business and employ others, you'll already know how accidents and illness can impact your organization and your bottom line. If you're an employee, you'll almost certainly have either been a victim yourself or will know of someone else who has.

This is my point: Safety at work is a two-way activity. It affects two groups – the owner and the employees.

Business owners certainly have a responsibility for complying with health and safety laws and going beyond that to protect the welfare of employees (and visiting customers). But employees have a duty of care, too—in their own interests, to protect their health and earning capacity, as well as that of colleagues and the business. It's a team thing comprising the company and employees working together in a safe manner: A dynamic duo!

There are whole sets of manuals and numerous Government and other agencies whose principal focus is the subject of business health and safety, and, these days, there are masses of information readily available online.

My plan is to highlight the key areas where you can make a significant impact on workplace safety for the benefit of all. These include the things you absolutely must do, plus additional actions I recommend from a lifetime of contact with small businesses.

KNOW THE LAW

Health and safety legislation is churned out by the bucket-load, and it can be difficult and time-consuming to keep track of what affects you and what doesn't. The 1970 Occupational Safety & Health Act (OSHA) is the main federal law on the subject. Its declared aim is "to assure so far as possible every working man and woman in the Nation safe and healthful working conditions and to preserve our human resources."

This is a huge document, but the Department of Labor publishes a useful summary online.

In addition, your state and local governments will have regulations dealing with your specific type of business. Most states have their own division of the Occupational Safety & Health Administration (also abbreviated as OSHA), sometimes with additional laws tacked on.

Your state Attorney General's Office and, if they have one, the Department of Business Affairs can also provide information on state legislation. Locally, your county or city administrations will be able to signpost any regulations that affect safety at your business.

That said, that's an awful lot of running-around-researching when you have a business to operate, so there are a number of shortcuts you can take to make sure you're clued in both to current requirements and upcoming changes.

I always recommend that clients have memberships for professional and trade organizations for their type of business and the local Chamber of

Commerce. They can provide additional guidance and resources. If you're not already a Chamber member, I advise that you sign up.

There are also numerous online groups offering business guidance and updates, and, these days, many states and regions operate Small Business Advisory Councils.

TOP 10 COMMONSENSE WORKPLACE SAFETY RULES

In addition to what the law says you should do to ensure a safer, healthier workplace, there are also what I call the Commonsense Rules. There are guidelines that simply make sense and which everyone should follow, employer and employee. Here are my Top 10:

1. **Remove or highlight hazards, and keep the place tidy and clean.**

   Most workplace injuries are caused by falls and collisions. If you apply that old adage—"a place for everything and everything in its place"— you'll significantly reduce the risk of this kind of accident.

   The same diligence applies to cleanliness. Sickness can be caused by poor bathroom, and kitchen hygiene and bacterial infection passed through shared items like phones. Post hand-washing notices and keep a ready supply of antibacterial wipes.

2. **Operate effective heating and ventilation.**

   OSHA does not set legal maximum or minimum levels for temperatures and humidity (though some states do). When you think of it, comfortable-temperature working conditions are a basic component of a good workplace. A good workplace is where the best, most productive workers hang out.

   The nature of the job may affect the temperatures in which you expect people to work. If you run a refrigerated store or industrial furnace, for example, your situation may be different than another business that doesn't. Your state OSHA can help, but a useful guideline outside the kind of extremes I just mentioned are working temperatures in the range of 68 to 76 degrees and a humidity range of 20 to 60 percent.

A word about cigarette smoke: Most states no longer permit smoking in public buildings and workplaces, except, rarely, in strictly controlled, designated areas. They often also ban smoking outside within a certain distance of doors and windows. We all know that smoking is dangerous to health, and since you know that, employees could try to hold you liable for any health problems they suffer because of others' smoking.

3. **Have the right safety equipment.**

    By that, I mean keep a well-stocked First Aid kit, and have on hand fire extinguishers and blankets, fire, smoke, and carbon monoxide alarms, and any special products needed to deal with hazards specifically related to your type of business.

    You should also consider having emergency resuscitation equipment, such as a portable Automatic External Defibrillator (AED).

    But just having these items isn't enough. Regularly checking and maintaining them, and, in the case of things like fire extinguishers, training people to use them properly, is a must. So…

    Provide or acquire safety skills and understanding. You should always have at least one qualified First Aider in your business. If you don't, either get the training for yourself or pay for one or more employees to take the courses.

    That's only the start. It's important that everyone in your workplace understands and buys into your commitment to a safe workplace.

Achieve this by having a written safety code (this list might be a good start!) and making it clear that compliance is mandatory.

4. **Store dangerous materials properly.**

I'm not just talking to businesses that use chemicals. Everything that's flammable, potentially poisonous, or noxious, like cleaning fluids and maintenance materials, as well as sharp implements like scissors and blades, should be properly labeled and stored under lock and key, with clear instructions on how they must be handled.

5. **Have the right clothes for the job.**

Wear protective clothing designed for the job, from steel toecap shoes and hard-hat helmets to eye protection, safety gloves, and everything in between.

Even in an office environment, some tasks, like changing the toner on a copier or making temporary repairs to broken equipment or furniture, might require the use of protective gear.

6. **Treat others and equipment with respect.**

Any hint of workplace violence or other abusive behavior should be curtailed immediately, with a clear warning of disciplinary action.

Encourage employees and fellow workers to show special consideration for those less physically able and to alert others when a danger is spotted. Take care when you're opening doors. Do you know who's on the other side?

Your business equipment deserves the same respect. No liquids near PCs and other electrical equipment, caution when using sharp items or replacing blades, and make sure you power equipment off when not in use. Treat cutting blades as what they are—potentially lethal weapons.

7. **Have an emergency plan and conduct regular safety drills for the sort of emergencies that might occur in your workplace.**

This plan should be written down, regularly reviewed, and updated. The sad fact is that most firms don't have such a plan, and when disaster strikes, they wish they did. They're totally unprepared.

8. **Be aware of health issues in the workplace and act quickly to deal with contagious sickness.**

Okay, you can't go snooping around, but you can use your eyes and ears to pick up issues that suggest a health problem. This could be anything from colds or flu to a more serious problem that, by affecting an individual's performance, poses a safety risk.

You need to encourage an open and honest working environment where people feel safe to talk about these things. And you need to make it clear that you don't want heroes who come into work when they're sick and pass around their germs. Have a system that enables these people to work from home if they want to. Workplace stress is another increasingly important health issue.

9. **Protect your stuff—and your staff.**

Someone could break into your business, injure themselves then sue you. Believe me; it's happened.

But I'm more concerned about the security of your employees, your equipment, and anything else you store in the building. This is especially important if you run a business that regularly interacts with the public and/or keeps significant money or other valuables on the premises.

If you do, you probably already have security alarms and cameras installed, and hopefully, you've told your employees never to mess with a robber. Just give him (or her) the money! If you haven't, have that talk now. Always keep hazardous materials locked away, particularly items that could cause damage if they fell into the wrong hands.

The basic rule is to do all you can to stop would-be intruders. By doing so, you could save on your insurance, too.

10. Keep a record

This is more of an action, but it's just as essential: Keep a record of incidents, complaints, equipment installations, employee suggestions, training programs, and disaster action and recovery plans. Doing this means you will always be familiar with your safety programs and policies and what needs to be done next. It also means you will have written documentation that you may need for legal purposes—either in connection with the enforcement of regulations or—and I hope this doesn't happen—if your liability is being tested in court.

You may have others to add. That's all right. The key point is that everyone knows them and that they are written down, circulated to employees (especially newcomers) and customers, and regularly reviewed. Now let's examine some of these points in more detail.

KNOW WHAT YOUR EMPLOYEES KNOW

This is both a question and a statement. Do you know what your employees think about workplace health and safety? If not, you'd better find out. Even in the smallest of businesses, everyone should have an awareness of these issues. Just maybe they'll have some good ideas that could make your workplace safer.

You can test for both of these things by doing a survey. This doesn't have to be a formal, splashy affair, but it will provide you with valuable feedback at the same time as it signals your commitment to their safety and well-being while underlining their shared responsibility.

You want to establish if they are aware of your policy, that they know how and where to get any relevant information, where equipment and protective wear is stored, and who to go to for first aid.

Do they know how to report workplace accidents, and are they aware of any that have gone unreported? Do they understand how to safely operate job-related equipment or feel they need training in any aspect of safety? Finally, do they have concerns (for example, about heating, lighting, ergonomics) or suggestions to make about any aspect of safety at work?

If you can do this, in association with the guidelines I've provided above, you will be well on your way to reducing the risk of accidents at work —and raising productivity!

BE PREPARED: EMERGENCY PLANNING

The same sort of disasters that can befall a home apply to the workplace, with potentially even more serious consequences, not just because of the number of people affected but also because some companies have additional hazards that could create emergencies.

In addition to the risk to human life, there's the threat to the continuity of your business and the livelihood of your employees and you!

Check out the IBHS (Insurance Institute for Business & Home Safety) site, disastersafety.org. You'll find some good tips on various hazard risks and programs dealing with them.

One of the best sources of information for disaster planning in all aspects of life, including business, is the National Safety Council (NSC), which offers a vast array of print information to its members as well as a huge library of online resources, including its own "readiness assessment."

Emergency planning doesn't have to be a daunting task to tackle. It can easily be accomplished if you reduce it to bite-size chunks. If your company is large enough, and if you nominate someone (at a senior level) to take ownership of it, all the better.

As NSC points out, current legislation for this kind of planning is covered by OSHA, but many of the standards of the governing law are largely out of date and provide no comprehensive plan that covers the whole range of emergencies that can arise in business. So that's going to be your job!

According to NSC, an emergency response plan should be developed locally and be comprehensive enough to deal with all types of emergencies specific to that facility.

When emergency action plans are required by a particular OSHA standard, the plan must be in writing, except for firms with 10 or fewer employees, where the plan may be communicated orally to employees.

The purpose of the plan is to identify the possible risks to the safety of your people and your business, who has responsibility for what, the different aspects of managing each type of emergency, the actions to be taken, and how communications will work.

I suggest you set a timetable for putting this together and, once it's complete, for putting it into practice. If you join NSC, you can also download an emergency planning template and a drills-and-training exercise plan. For further advice, the organization has chapters in most states.

I can't stress enough the importance of testing the procedures you develop for your emergency plan. If I were a gambler, I would wager a sizeable bet that when you do test it, you'll discover a number of flaws both in the plan itself and in people being aware of what to do. Use this experience to refine the plan and the associated learning.

In addition to the peace of mind, you'll get from having a workable plan, there's another great benefit: The opportunity to take actions that reduce the risks you've identified.

This should be an ongoing process, with a written action plan that results in continuous improvement in the health and safety of your workplace.

TAKING THE STRESS OUT OF STRESS

You know that feeling when you've "had it up to here"? Of course, you do; everyone does, whether you're an owner or employee. Stress has become a major factor in workplace sickness during the past couple of decades.

With the pace of doing business accelerating almost by the day, I imagine the issue will only become more acute. The result is usually personal misery, extreme loss of productivity, and sometimes, poor decision-making.

It makes sense to have a simple stress management policy in place. This involves taking action to reduce the likelihood of stress, recognizing the signals when it does occur, facing the issue, and helping with the healing process.

The plain fact is that each of us has a different level of stress resistance and a different mechanism for coping with it, so there's no "one-size-fits-all" solution.

According to the National Institute of Occupational Safety and Health (NIOSH), early warning signs of job stress include headache, sleep disturbances, difficulty concentrating, short temper, upset stomach, job dissatisfaction, and low morale.

Sheesh! I've suffered most of those myself—well, maybe not the last two, as I've always made a point of doing a job I enjoy. The important aspect is to recognize when you, or another person, suffers these symptoms often and for prolonged periods.

If they are not spotted and dealt with, they could increase the risk of cardiovascular disease, back and shoulder disorders, severe psychological problems, workplace injury (of course), and in the worst-case scenarios, cancers, and even suicide.

As noted in *American Psychologist* magazine, NIOSH offers the following tips for preventing job stress:

1. Ensure that the workload is in line with workers' capabilities and resources.

2. Design jobs to provide meaning, stimulation, and opportunities for workers to use their skills.

3. Clearly define workers' roles and responsibilities.

4. Give employees opportunities to participate in decisions and actions affecting their jobs.

5. Improve communications – Reduce uncertainty about career development and future employment prospects.

6. Provide opportunities for social interaction among employees.

7. Establish work schedules that are compatible with demands and responsibilities outside the job.

To that, I'd add the importance of creating a healthy work environment and ensuring everyone takes breaks, including screen breaks, days off, and vacations at the appropriate time, no matter how busy you are. That means you as well!

If you suspect that you are or another person is suffering from stress, then you or that person needs to seek professional help; it's beyond the scope of this book to offer meaningful, effective suggestions. But, whatever you do, don't shrug it off. Stress is real, and it can be a killer.

ENVIRONMENTAL ISSUES

I've already mentioned the issue of cigarette smoke in or near the workplace. Happily, most employees are now in sync with the rules, although it still drives me nuts when I go to enter a building and have to pass through a haze of smoke, and a horde of fast-puffing employees, while stepping over a mound of cigarette butts.

That said, there are also a number of less visible environmental issues, all with potentially harmful consequences to business.

1. **Asbestos**

   These days, most asbestos, which was used so heavily as a fire retardant in the early and mid-part of the 20th century, has been identified and removed. Still, the US Department of Labor reckons more than a million workers, mainly in the construction industry, remain exposed to it.

   If you suspect there may be asbestos in your business premises, you need to arrange an inspection by a certified and licensed specialist. Find them online or in the phone book, and make sure you check their credentials.

2. **Lead**

   In addition to being a big public health risk, over-exposure to lead in the workplace is a major cause of job sickness. You might find it in paint, dust, food, water, and even in the air. Lead poisoning gives rise to a variety of blood and digestion-related disorders.

   Common symptoms of acute lead poisoning are, according to OSHA, loss of appetite, nausea, vomiting, stomach cramps, constipation, difficulty sleeping, fatigue, moodiness, headache, joint or muscle aches, anemia, and decreased sexual drive.

The best way to protect workers is to minimize their exposure where you know risks exist and to use protective clothing and respirators when required. If the symptoms I've described emerge, they should see a doctor.

3. Allergens

I hate that moment in the doctor's or dentist's office when they ask if I'm allergic to latex gloves. Something painful is sure to follow. It turns out that millions of Americans are allergic to latex and that it is much more widely used than just in surgeries.

Plus, they're just one of many products that cause allergies. A friend, for instance, is not allergic to latex but can't eat kiwi fruit without it causing a terrible itching in his throat.

Just make a point of knowing any allergies that anyone in your business has and make sure they don't come into contact with the offending products. If it's a seasonal allergy (rhinitis), consider installing a pollen filter on your a/c system.

4. Confined spaces

Just because you don't panic if the elevator gets stuck doesn't mean everyone in your workplace feels the same. Claustrophobia is a big issue at work, and as office cubicles shrink, the issues with it will grow.

Again, the key preventative measure is to establish if this is an issue for any of your employees and to make sure they're comfortable with their workstation location. Oftentimes, people won't fess up to this disorder until they experience a panic attack. It's a contributor to stress and disharmony, so do all you can to avoid it.

FINALLY...

Please, again, check the final chapter in this book to discover how insurance and insurers can help you in your quest to maximize workplace safety and employee contentment. You could cut your premiums, improve morale, and literally profit from the experience!

CHAPTER FIVE

SAFETY ON WHEELS—AND ON FOOT

Here's a quick quiz: Name 10 occasions when it's unsafe to be on the road. I'm not just talking to car drivers here, but also cyclists and even pedestrians.

You almost need to cover your eyes and peek between your fingers when I give you the facts.

Did you know that someone dies on our roads every 13 minutes?[1] In fact, since January 2000, more Americans have been killed in traffic accidents than have lost their lives in both World Wars.[2] There are more than six million accidents a year on US roads, a third of them resulting in injury.[3]

Around the world, more than a million people die on the roads every year[4], and another 50 million are injured.[5] Likely every one of them imagined an accident would never happen to them. Please don't be complacent.

As someone once famously said, "Accidents don't happen; they're caused." This can be a good thing because it means, in many cases, there's something you can do about it. You can avoid the situations where you might be the cause, or you can prepare yourself for potential hazards imposed by others, like a deer that jumps into your path or a car that careens out of control towards you.

---

[1] https://www.thewanderingrv.com/car-accident-statistics/
[2] https://www.washingtonpost.com/local/trafficandcommuting/more-people-died-in-car-crashes-this-century-than-in-both-world-wars/2019/07/21/0ecc0006-3f54-11e9-9361-301ffb5bd5e6_story.html
[3] https://www.driverknowledge.com/car-accident-statistics/
[4] https://www.cdc.gov/injury/features/global-road-safety/index.html
[5] https://www.asirt.org/safe-travel/road-safety-facts/

ACCIDENT LOCATIONS

When you're out and about, it's worth knowing the danger spots, aka, the places where accidents are most likely to occur. For instance, many car mishaps happen within a short distance of home (which is why it's so important to belt up as soon as you get in your vehicle).

Roads in built-up areas are more likely the scene of an accident than a major highway or freeway, and most rear-end collisions happen at intersections (both signaled and unsignaled) or in traffic snarls.

Two-way roads with a single lane in each direction and with no physical division down the center are the most likely place for a head-on collision, especially at bends. Out-of-town streets, which tend to be most twisty and where motorists might drive faster, have the highest risk of all.

SIMPLE SAFE DRIVING RULES

If you know, from the previous section, where accidents are most likely to occur, it stands to reason that those are the places where you should exercise the most caution. Following other simple driving rules will further greatly reduce the risk of a crash.

- Avoid driving when you are tired – Drinking caffeinated drinks and eating sugary snacks can help you stay alert, but only in the short term. Take a rest break, with exercise, every couple of hours. Remember, there's only one true solution when you're tired. Stop and sleep.

- Always drive within the speed limit. These limits may frustrate us, but they're there for a purpose beyond raising revenue for the police department.

- Even within the speed limit, driving too fast for the road conditions increases anxiety and causes crashes.

- Don't drink (or take drugs) and drive. Everyone knows this rule, but so many people ignore it. There's strong evidence to suggest there's no such thing as a "safe" level of alcohol for drivers. Just don't do it.

- Practice courtesy. I talk about road rage a little later, but there's a level below that, which leads to numerous traffic incidents. It happens most when you assume you have the right of way ... but ... so does the other driver.

- You could be at a four-way stop, pulling out from a parking bay, or planning a maneuver, like passing another vehicle. Giving way to the other driver is not only safer; it'll also make you feel good!

- Keep your auto clean and in good health - Dirty windows equal poor visibility. Add in poor brakes, lighting, windshield wipers, door locks, tire condition, and pressures, and you're mixing a recipe for disaster. Good maintenance not only enhances vehicle safety but, in the long term, it probably saves you money.

- Park and drive off with care, checking all mirrors and looking over your shoulder where necessary. Check mirrors for pedestrians and cyclists when opening your car door.

THINK ABOUT THE KIDS

- According to the National Road Safety Foundation, car crashes are the leading cause of death for children ages 5 to 14. Half of these fatalities were unrestrained, neither wearing seat belts or in a child safety seat.

- Kids also should not go in rear-facing child seats on the front seat of cars that have passenger-side airbags. On the rear seat, position them away from the expansion area of a deploying airbag. Adults should never hold children on their laps.

- Child safety in cars isn't just about seating kids correctly. It's also about keeping them under control. Distractions inside a car are another major cause of road accidents. This includes kids who are fighting or arguing while you are trying to drive—especially if you are in a hurry to get them to school, scouts, or wherever.

- This is a matter of personal discipline, but also, some children are just naturally more boisterous than others. You need a safety code that they understand and buy into—like stopping the journey and waiting until they calm down or imposing sanctions for their misbehavior. It's tough, but it could save their lives and yours.

- Never forget about the children who are not inside the car either. Children don't share the sense of danger adults have. Even when they're older, they may simply be too distracted—texting with friends, for instance—and walk straight into the path of danger.

- Keep an extra sharp eye on the roads and sidewalks when kids are about. As a parent, never lose the opportunity to alert them to dangers and develop their road sense.

Which leads me to....

YOUNG DRIVERS

I'll bet you can remember when you first sat behind the wheel of a car, or, if not when you first drove solo or got your first car.

It's a landmark on the road to adulthood. But, if you were anything like me, you weren't an adult and sometimes failed to observe all the common-sense rules and driving skills you should have acquired.

Sadly, too, I can think of more than one occasion when I read in my local newspaper of a teen car tragedy that often resulted from high spirits, especially after graduation, and sometimes even real spirits—alcohol.

So, here are guidelines for safe teen driving. It's your job to convince the young drivers in your life of their wisdom.

- Learners should have instruction from drivers who are as experienced as possible—preferably professional instructors using a special, marked learner vehicle.

- Allow few or no passengers in the car when your teen is driving, especially at night, when extra caution should also be exercised.

- Do not let them drive any high-performance vehicles—either yours or their own. No racing.

- Wear seatbelts at all times.

I think it's also a good idea for young drivers to pay for or contribute to their own vehicle insurance so they have an appreciation of the cost and risks of teenage driving.

The NHTSA has some excellent source material on teen driving on its website, including a useful Parental Responsibility Toolkit.

SENIORS

There comes a point when it's time to stop driving. That age varies tremendously according to an individual's state of vision and physical and mental agility. The trouble is that most older folk either don't recognize this point or don't want to face it.

If you are a senior or know someone who is, no matter how young and fit you/they feel, it's time to start monitoring driving performance.

The symptoms of age-related driving impairment are easy to spot: Persistent tiredness, poor vision and/or hearing, confusion about rules and direction, slowing reflexes when braking, unstable steering.

Many states now check for these issues by requiring re-testing for a driver's license after a certain age. But the frequency of these re-tests generally is not enough to identify the fairly sudden onset of these conditions.

If you are advancing in years, I recommend that you discuss your driving suitability with your doctor when you have your annual physical and that you listen to any concerns expressed by friends and family. If it's time to hang up your keys, have the courage to do so. It's in your own interest.

If you're younger but have older parents or other relatives whose driving skills have become questionable, I urge you to raise the issue straightaway. But do it with compassion, and only after you devise a plan to help them out with their mobility needs.

ROAD CONDITIONS AND ROAD GEAR

When you're heading out onto the open road, whether on foot or on wheels, it pays to think about the conditions you're going to face and any special protection you might need.

Don't forget, too, that the law requires certain items, like helmets and lights for cyclists and motorcyclists in most states.

If it's dark or likely to darken while you're out, follow these rules:

- Don't drive if you have night vision problems (but you can get some corrective glasses for mild conditions), and have or wear high-visibility clothing so you can easily be spotted by other drivers when you're on foot or on a cycle. Drivers should also carry illuminated warning triangles that can be set up in the event of a breakdown or accident.

- If floods or severe storms threaten your journey, reconsider if it's really necessary to go out. If you do go, take waterproof gear and a cell phone.

- If it's possible your journey could leave you stranded for any length of time, pack food and water, plus extra clothing. Keep your gas tank full, so you can stay warm.

THE RAGE STAGE

Who hasn't sat behind a dawdling driver or been harassed by an impatient tailgater and felt like wringing the neck of the offender? Judge me guilty on that count. I confess to muttering a few choice words under my breath, although I never did go beyond that!

Or how about when you get flipped off or honked at by another aggressive driver just because you made a simple driving error, or maybe when you did nothing wrong at all? Been there, done that too?

Then you won't be surprised that, according to road safety experts, around half of all auto accidents involve some kind of aggressive driving. I don't know about you, but I sense the problem is getting worse as our roads get busier and the pace of life speeds up.

If you're inclined to be aggressive, impatient, intolerant, or otherwise unworthy of being behind a steering wheel because of your mood, the most important action you can take is to avoid speeding and allow yourself plenty of time to get to your destination.

Safety experts say it also helps to have food in the car to snack on and to mentally force yourself to relax. Monitor your body for tension and try to let it go. But please don't eat and drive.

If, on the other hand, you're on the receiving end of another driver's aggression, here are some things you should and shouldn't do:

- Stay calm. Two wrongs won't make it right.

- Don't be pressured into breaking a speed limit.

- Avoid eye contact with the aggressor, either directly or via your mirrors.

- If they are harassing you, pull over and let them pass.

- If they get out of the car and threaten you, keep your window shut.

- If you're involved in an accident or otherwise intimidated by them, call 911.

CELL PHONES, PETS, AND OTHER DISTRACTIONS

Safe driving calls for two hands on the wheel, two eyes on the road, and one brain fully focused on the task. Multi-tasking, so much a part of our busy lives these days, is not a wise option when you're driving.

That's why many states have now outlawed the use of hand-held cell phones. But here's an interesting thing: research suggests that hands-free phones, which everyone is switching to, are hardly any safer. In some parts of Europe, they are banned. I can see that happening here in the US in time as these findings are confirmed.

The fact is that talking to another person, either by phone or even directly when they're a passenger in your car, demands a degree of concentration, and that has to come from somewhere.

Answer: It comes from the concentration you'd otherwise be devoting to your driving. In other words, talking, at least in the form of prolonged conversation, is a distraction that affects your safety.

I've already mentioned the impact of boisterous children on your concentration. The same goes for rowdy pets, usually dogs, that excitedly bounce around the inside of your vehicle, and in the worst case, bark incessantly.

These and other distractions need to be controlled or eliminated. My advice is not to use a cell phone at all while you are driving. If you have a hands-free setup, by all means, answer it if the law permits you to, and then either pull off the road (if it's safe to do) or tell the other party that you'll call back.

Obviously, *never, never* try to send a text message while driving. In most states, it's now illegal, but to try to do it anyway, anywhere, is just plain crazy.

Just as important, if you have teen drivers in your house (who seem to have an umbilical connection to their cell phones), please impress this safety code on them.

As for other distractions, unfortunately, while you might be able to control excitable kids in the car, it's not such an easy task with pets, but there are four things you can do to lessen the distraction factor while in the car.

POINTERS FOR DRIVING WITH PETS

- Always keep pets in the back of the vehicle, never in the front, and absolutely, never on your lap when you're driving.

- Tether them with a short harness so they can't bounce around.

- Muzzle them so they can't bark—at least with full force.

- Preferably, have a passenger in the back with them who can both calm and control them.

If you have a particularly lively dog, you need to rethink your strategy of taking it with you when you go out. Wouldn't it—and you—be better off if the animal stayed at home?

SAFETY ON TWO WHEELS

It's great to see more and more cities providing separate roadside lanes for cyclists, isn't it? More people are hitting the road on two wheels—whether on bikes or motorcycles—as a simpler, more environmentally considerate, and cost-effective way of getting around.

But let's be clear; it's not a safer way to travel. Two wheels are less stable than four, and the narrowness of the transport can both tempt you to take road risks in heavy traffic and render you less visible to others on the road.

CYCLE SAFETY

I like the advice that award-winning writer Michael Bluejay gives when he says, "Ride as if you are invisible."

He explains: "It's often helpful to ride in such a way that motorists won't hit you even if they don't see you. You're not trying to be invisible; you're trying to make it irrelevant whether cars see you or not. If you stay out of their way, then you won't get hit even if they didn't notice you were there."

It's worth checking out Michael's site, which teems with tips for safer cycling. He lists multiple ways not to get hit, and other useful information but his key safety points are to use a headlight (required by law at night anyway), get and use a horn and a rear-view mirror, slow down when you see a potential hazard, don't ride on the sidewalk or against traffic, never stop in a driver's "blind spot," don't pass a vehicle on the right at an intersection (in case it turns right), don't hug the curb and never move out (to the left) without looking behind you.

Of course, always wear a safety helmet.

MOTORCYCLE SAFETY

Motorcycling is a hobby—a passion, even—for an increasing number of people. Unfortunately, most of these people tend to be less experienced than full-time riders and therefore, they are more vulnerable to accidents.

My first rule: Never ride a motorcycle without using a helmet. That goes for passengers, too. Anyway, it's the law! Many of the guidelines for road safety, including those for car drivers, cyclists (especially the visibility issue), and road rage, apply equally to motorcyclists. But here are a few more:

- Get proper training and get your license.

- Wear protective, high visibility gear at all times, including reflective strips for night riding.

- Get to know your vehicle, understand braking techniques, and perform a safety check before each trip.

- Be especially wary of adverse weather. Slow down in rain, or even stop if it becomes torrential. Both your stability and visibility are threatened in these conditions.

Before I sign off on this issue, let me point out that although I've been talking to bikers in this section, it's just as important for car drivers to be aware of the vulnerability of this group of road users and to exercise extreme caution and courtesy when they're around.

ACCIDENT SCENE ACTIONS

If you're involved in an accident of any sort, the first step is to resist any temptation not to stop (or you'll be breaking the law). If it causes personal injury or serious damage to vehicles, get clear of the vehicle (if possible), and call 911.

In fact, in all but the most minor of bumps, you should always contact the police or at least report the incident within 24 hours.

What you do next depends on the nature of the accident, but always try to stay calm and first check the condition of everyone involved.

If someone is injured and you can give first aid, do so, provided you know what you are doing, especially in relation to the risks of moving injured people (basically, don't move an injured person unless they're in range of a potential fire, explosion, or other danger). Ideally, you should carry an emergency First Aid kit in the car at all times. You may need it yourself. Then, follow these guidelines:

- If possible, set up emergency triangles to warn other drivers of the hazard.

- Identify any witnesses who might have seen the accident, collecting names and addresses.

- Do not discuss the accident or the issue of blame with anyone. Never admit it was your fault, even if you know it was.

- If you have a camera and feel up to it, take photographs of damage and vehicle positions.

- Exchange insurance, vehicle registration, license, and contact details with any other driver involved.

- Jot down any other details of what you recall from the incident, like weather conditions, driving speed, and what happened. You might have trouble recalling them later.

- If it's safe to do so, and you have police permission, move your vehicle off the street or highway. If it's not drivable, tow-truck removal is usually your responsibility.

- Contact your agent or insurer and file an accident report.

- Prepare for and deal with after-effects. You may just be badly shaken, or you could have an injury that won't materialize until sometime later. Get a medical check-up.

Following these guidelines is particularly important from the auto insurance point of view, so let's quickly rewind to the start of this section—here's an important tip for you to do right now.

Take a look at your auto policy and check what your insurer advises you to do after a collision. Mostly, they'll follow the pointers I've given here, but you need to know if there are any additional, special requirements.

Your policy documents may also include an accident report form. Put this in your car, so you can use it if you're unfortunate as to be involved in a crash.

SHOWING THE WAY FOR PEDESTRIANS

No, I didn't forget road safety for those folk who are on foot rather than wheels. The risk of injury is high when three tons of metal collide with a human body, but, contrary to what you might expect, the most frequent cause of these accidents is pedestrian rather than driver error.

There's no way you can guarantee avoiding such a mishap, but you can substantially reduce the risk by being vigilant, especially in busy traffic areas. I don't want to spoil the party but, personally, I'm against wearing headphones and listening to music in busy urban traffic areas, for instance.

Here are some more pointers:

- If there's a sidewalk, don't walk on the street or near the edge of the sidewalk. If there's no sidewalk, keep to the edge of the street and walk against the flow of traffic so you can see what's coming toward you.

- Cross at marked crossings and intersections, never assuming that any traffic heading in your direction is going to see you and stop, even if you have a light signal in your favor. Be especially wary if you have to emerge from between parked vehicles to cross the street.

- If you have young children with you, hold their hands—even against their inevitable protests—and use every opportunity to teach them road sense.

- It's a good idea to walk them through your neighborhood to help identify risks and work out safe routes. You might even spot potential hazards you can raise with your city to improve local road safety.

- Don't go out on a busy street if you feel dizzy, confused, or if you are under the influence of drugs or alcohol. More than a third of pedestrians killed in road accidents have significantly elevated blood alcohol levels.

- At night, wear high visibility, reflective clothing, and even consider carrying a flashlight. You can buy battery-powered LED (light-emitting diode) lights that attach to your sleeve or belt and that flash on and off.

- An important point that people often overlook: Use additional caution when you're in an unfamiliar place, especially in another country, where driving and parking behavior might be quite different than what you are used to.

CHAPTER SIX

MAKE SURE IT'S A BON VOYAGE (GOOD TRIP!)

A few years ago, a friend made a business trip to Italy with a hectic schedule of pre-arranged meetings. It was his first visit to that beautiful country, and he was about a half-an-hour into his rental car journey from the airport to his first destination when he realized he had left his cell phone on the plane.

Every single appointment he had made and all the background information he needed was on that thing, and there he was on the autostrada, in rush-hour traffic, heading away from it as fast as he could.

He slipped down an off-ramp, planning to do a U-turn and head back toward the airport, only to discover there was no matching on-ramp. He was lost, didn't speak the lingo, and had no backup for the data on his cell phone.

Long story short, he eventually got back to the airport through a process of trial and error, hand-waving, and shrugging, then parked illegally (although he didn't know it at the time) and raced back inside.

The desk of the airline he had flown with was shut, and the gal at the information kiosk could only suggest he go to the Lost & Found booth. Where was that? Why, in the baggage reclaim—on the other side of a couple of burly, armed Carabinieri.

Then, he noticed that people were walking in and out of this area without them even blinking (believe it or not, this was post 9/11), so he gave it a try, got to Lost & Found, and, to his utter relief, discovered that the cabin crew had found his cell phone and handed it in. "Here it is. Just sign here," The person behind the counter said. "Oh, and don't forget to pay that parking ticket."

He's a seasoned and cautious traveler and, these days, a lot wiser, but his experience reminded me of some critical lessons that everyone should remember when traveling, especially to an unfamiliar, foreign country:

- Always back up your important information.

- Don't assume the road system works the same way it does in the US. Italian drivers, by the way, are notoriously competitive.

- Learn a few key phrases, like "Which way to the airport?"; and road signs like "No parking."

- Realize that cultures are different and that, for better or worse, security procedures might not match your expectations.

- Always check the seat pockets and baggage compartments before you deplane. *Sheesh, he still can't believe he forgot that!*

What's your travel confession? Because I'd be 100% disbelieving if you claimed you'd never made a mistake, learned a lesson, got sick, or ended up in some kind of jam while you were away from home.

Hopefully, though, what I'm going to explain will help you steer clear of the more common health and safety issues you might encounter on vacation or business trips, not just in other countries but also here in the US.

TRAVEL TIPS NOTES

Don't you just love it when you pick up your newspaper or tune in to the local TV station and hear good news? They usually dole out so much of the bad stuff that it's easy to get the idea that that's how life is.

It's the same with travel: Although everyone has a tale of woe, whether it's a mile-long line at airport security or a typhoid outbreak at your hotel (been there, too), the fact is that most people experience trouble-free travel and vacations, most of the time.

You can increase your chances of being in that category with my Travel Tips Notes. This list covers generalities, whether you're in the US or another country.

Later, we'll look more closely at international travel, as well as special needs, scams, and the very important issue of insurance.

Let's get started.

PLANNING BEGINS AT HOME

You can't have a great vacation if you spend your time worrying about the security of your home. People who might need to contact you will have a bad time if they don't know where you are. Here's a checklist of things to do:

❑ Make a copy of your itinerary, with contact details, and give it, with a key and information on where important documents, like wills, are to be found, to a relative or acquaintance you trust.

❑ Let a close neighbor you trust know you're leaving and ask them to keep an eye on your home. They can also watch out for doorstep package deliveries and put out your trash can.

❑ Cancel your newspapers and hold your mail. It's easy to order a mail hold online or by phoning your local USPS customer service branch.

❑ Make it look like you're still home. Arrange for your lawns to be mowed, and gardens tended and set up timers to switch lights on and off.

❑ Know where it's at. Thanks to the internet, it's so easy these days to find all the information you might need about the place(s) you're staying and visiting. The best time to acquire that knowledge is before you leave.

❑ Do a search on the name of your location. Download maps, check out medical facilities, and the police department. Learn about things to do, as well as about the unsafe areas.

❑ Even if you don't have an Internet connection, phone the tourist office or your hotel, asking for brochures and maps. Buy or order a street map from your local bookstore.

❑ Be prepared. Here's a must-have list to start you off:

- Know where all your documents are – such as travel tickets, hotel confirmations, passports.
- Have a contact list in case you need to get in touch with people back home.
- Bring enough prescription medications for the time you're away, plus a few spares.
- Includes a travel first aid kit, a sewing repair kit, a small flashlight, and a penknife (this must go in your checked baggage if you're flying).
- If you wear reading glasses, take a spare pair.
- Pack weather-appropriate clothing. If you're flying, put a spare set of essential clothing, like underwear, in your hand baggage, in case your luggage gets lost.
- Don't forget spare batteries and/or rechargers for electronic equipment.
- Bring with you a note of serial numbers of any valuable items you plan to take – like cameras and notebook PCs.

But…

- Leave other valuables and spare credit cards in a home safe or safety deposit box.
- Travel light. It's easier to move around in busy places.

❑ A safe base: When researching your hotel or vacation rental, do these three important things: 1) make sure it's well located for the amenities you want; 2) check if it's in a crime-risk area; and 3) if you have internet, read others' reviews of the property and locale.

❑ When you arrive, get to know the safety regulations, including escape routes. Don't leave valuable stuff in your accommodation (unless it's in a safe), and keep the door locked at all times.

❑ If you're traveling with other people, ensure they all know how to get back to the hotel in case you become separated while away.

❑ Here's an additional useful tip about hotel safety: Try to get a room between the second and seventh floors—out of reach of intruders but within reach of fire rescue.

❑ Be cautious when you're on the move. This isn't just about your driving, but others' too. There are lots of tips on road safety, but when you're traveling away from home, here are a few more things to consider:

- If you're renting a car, use established reputable agencies. Renting from unknowns is fraught with risks.

- If you use GPS satellite navigation, remember that it's not infallible, especially in remote areas. Buy a map. It's also a good idea to download an offline map in case you don't have cell service. Most importantly, stop and try to backtrack if you sense you are heading into trouble.

- Establish if local driving rules differ from the ones you're used to— for instance, can you still turn right at a red traffic signal or use cell phones while you're driving?

- Keep your car doors locked while driving, especially in built-up areas, and don't stop for hitch-hikers.

- If you're based in a built-up area, especially a city with one-way streets, make time to explore and get to know the road system when it's quiet.

- If your car breaks down, be cautious about accepting help from strangers. If the vehicle is not totally disabled, with a puncture, say, try to get to a gas station or some other well-lit public area.

- If you're planning to use a taxi, Uber, or Lyft, if possible, pre-book it. At airports and stations, only use clearly marked areas. Check approximate fares to your destination (compare them online before you go, if you can) and that the meter is reset to zero before the taxi pulls off.

- Traveling by bus? For security, choose a seat near to the driver, and if there's a seatbelt, wear it. By ferry? If you're the car driver, ensure you're comfortable making the tight maneuvers you may be asked to perform. If you're not a good sailor, take anti-nausea medication.

- Going by train? Don't get on or off when it's moving; watch your luggage at all times, and keep your wallet out of reach. Busy trains, especially subways, are a favorite haunt of pickpockets.

- Off the beaten path. I like to hike, laze on the beach, and explore the local sights. That's it. But some people are more adventurous and enjoy heading into the wilderness.

- If you're one of them, you probably already know the precautions, but, for novices, just let me point out that you should always let people know where you're going and carry a cell phone, waterproof and warm gear, a knife, high-energy food, water, and matches.

- Wearing correct footwear is vital—flimsy, slippery, and leaky shoes are a big cause of accidents and injury among inexperienced trekkers venturing into the wild.

- If you encounter a dangerous animal, stay calm. Don't run, but don't provoke it.

WORK WITH AIRPORT SECURITY

Let's just agree that air travel these days is a pain in the valise. But if you accept that there'll likely be long security lines and you'll be the one the TSA (Transport Security Administration) folk select for a random search—and you allow yourself plenty of time for this—you'll find getting through the airport a lot less trying.

These people are on your side, remember! But a couple of other important things:

- Watch your stuff as it emerges from the scanner. It's an old trick for a thief to walk off with it while you're waiting. Sometimes they have an accomplice who slows you down by getting caught in the body scanner.

- Second, in these days of terror alerts, you're probably safer on the secure side of the airport. After you check in, go to security, and get to the other side.

- Don't forget to ensure you comply with the rules laid down by TSA about what you can and can't travel with and what you're allowed to take in your hand luggage. The list is longer than you'd think, and there are a few surprises.

PERSONAL SAFETY
....

When you're in a place you don't know, it's just common sense to take extra care about where you go and what you eat and drink.

- For instance, it's advisable not to travel on foot alone at night, even in built-up areas where unscrupulous people might be looking for solo tourists.

- Never discuss your travel plans with someone you don't know. If you're confronted by a thief, don't resist. Give them money, etc., then report the incident to the police.

- Buying food and drink from street vendors in Third World countries is also inadvisable as it may not be prepared in hygienic conditions, and your digestive system won't be as resilient as theirs.

- Even buying bottled water may not be safe – get it at your hotel. On the other hand, in the US, buying bottled water at a convenience store may be cheaper than the hotel's prices.

- Take care of your health. Be aware of health issues in places you will visit. This doesn't just apply overseas. High altitude or humidity are important health considerations for some of us, so are allergy conditions, temperature extremes, and sun exposure, especially when you're not "acclimatized" to the place you're visiting.

- Dietary changes, even apparently harmless ones, can affect your digestive system, while prolonged travel, especially air travel, can lead to dehydration. For all the reasons in that preceding sentence, always drink plenty of good water on vacation.

INTERNATIONAL TRAVEL

New countries, new cultures, scenes of incredible beauty, strange but interesting ways of life, fascinating people, memorable experiences. Yes, they're all there. But make sure the lures of foreign travel don't become memorable for the wrong reasons.

Because our country is so vast, Americans are actually less experienced foreign travelers than, say, Europeans. We spend more vacation time in our own country, and perhaps we're less prepared for some of the challenges of traveling abroad.

Unfortunately, because of the high-profile global role the US plays—and the unfair perception that we're wealthy—Americans are sometimes resented or targeted by scammers.

Fortunately, our government goes to great lengths to protect its citizens abroad, and there's a vast amount of information available on everything from visa and inoculation requirements to what to do if an American is injured or dies abroad. Make sure to get the knowledge you need before you leave.

A good starting point is the State Department's Bureau of Consular Affairs website. Here's one of their Golden Rules you should always remember and let guide your actions:

"When you leave the United States, you are subject to the laws of the country you are visiting. Therefore, before you go, learn as much as you can about the local laws and customs of the places you plan to visit… In addition, keep track of what is being reported in the media about recent developments in those countries."

The Bureau maintains lists of countries for which there are alerts or no-travel advisories, guidance on how to deal with emergencies, and advice on getting or renewing a passport.

Particularly useful are country-specific pages allowing you to key in the name of the country you're visiting for details of entry requirements, currency regulations, unusual health conditions, crime and security, political disturbances, and driving and road conditions.

In addition to the tips I've listed, the Bureau also provides sound guidance on packing and what to take with you—like medicines (in hand baggage) in their original containers, with a letter from your physician if they contain narcotics; a spare set of passport photos with a copy of your passport information page; and your name, address, and telephone numbers inside and outside each piece of luggage (use covered luggage tags to keep them away from the eyes of snoopers).

The Bureau also recommends taking traveler's checks and credit cards instead of cash. Leave a list of the check numbers with someone back home that you can contact in an emergency, and ask your credit card company how to report a card loss when you're abroad.

You might consider getting a telephone calling card from a US service provider. This enables you to sidestep some of the complications of trying to work public phones that you're unfamiliar with. You can also check with your cell phone service provider on your options for adding an "abroad" plan, so you aren't blindsided by additional charges.

But, the Bureau recommends that you leave at home your social security card and other things you usually carry in your wallet but won't need for the trip, like library cards, for instance. If you lose your wallet, this will make your life a little easier when you get home.

Here's a useful tip that not a lot of people know about: You can actually register your journey with the State Department so you can be contacted in an emergency, and Uncle Sam knows where you are if trouble is looming.

This service is free and confidential (that is, the State Department won't release details of where you are to inquirers).

Beyond that, some other useful things you can do to improve safety and reduce risks when traveling abroad are:

- Buy a phrasebook and learn a few key terms before you go.

- Wear bags and cameras with shoulder straps across your chest.

- Find out and keep a note of the nearest US Embassy or consul location and phone number.

- Take only the money you need for an outing. Leave the rest, and a spare credit card, in the hotel safe.

- Don't sleep in a public place, especially with your baggage. Even on trains, this can be risky.

- Be wary of taking photos of official buildings. In some countries, this can put you behind bars.

- But if you need help, contact the local consular office. They can help with replacement passports, arranging medical care, putting you in touch with attorneys who speak English, and contacting family and employers in an emergency.

- If you have any doubts or questions about issues, restrictions, visas, etc., for any country, contact that country's embassy here in the US. The Department of State has a list of them all.

SPECIAL NEEDS

Some travelers have special health and safety needs beyond the points I've outlined. I'm thinking of women travelers (especially solo), pets, disabled people, the elderly, and children. Let's look at them one by one.

SAFER TRAVELING FOR WOMEN

- I'm not being sexist, honestly. Women travelers are definitely more at risk than men. They carry purses, wear jewelry, and may attract sexual predators.

- Avoiding solo night walks (use a taxi), carrying an audible alarm and pepper spray, keeping your hotel information confidential, dressing down, and avoiding elevators with just one male passenger are just a few useful tips to improve safety.

TRAVEL TIPS FOR PETS

- Traveling with a pet is usually not a problem within the US, but make sure to observe the advisories about keeping them hydrated and exercised along your journey.

- Hotels and airlines have different regulations about animals. To put it bluntly, some are more pet-friendly than others. Ensure that you check with them individually before booking.

- Research veterinary services before you go, and if your pet already has a health issue, check with your regular animal doc on the advisability of travel.

- Some resorts no longer allow pets on beaches or in public parks. Again, check before you go. If you plan to go abroad with your pet, check on restrictions, like quarantine, with the US-based embassy of the country you're visiting.

ASSISTANCE FOR DISABLED PEOPLE

Though they may be far from perfect, the US, Japan, Australia, and Western Europe have laws that ensure the minimum provision of services for people with disabilities—not so in other countries.

If you're disabled or there's a disabled person in your party, check out hotel facilities and how close your lodging is to amenities. If you have internet access, numerous specialist sites link to accommodations suitable for disabled folk.

The US Department of Transportation also publishes guidelines and pamphlets on air travel for disabled passengers.

WATCH THE KIDS

Don't let them out of your sight. Let me repeat that: Don't let children traveling with you out of your sight. Bustling tourist attractions and crowded beaches signal danger. Their minds wander, and so do they. Spend time alerting your kids to the dangers of getting lost and speaking to strangers, but have a backup plan that tells them what to do if you get separated.

Depending on their age, this might involve returning to an agreed-upon meeting place, or asking a person in uniform or a woman (not a man) for help.

CONSIDERATIONS FOR SENIORS

Once you reach a certain age (and it's different for all of us), you may not be as sharp-eyed or agile as you used to be. That can be an issue when you're traveling.

Plan appropriately, and select hotels and locations that might not be as taxing on your energy. Stay properly hydrated, avoid over-exertion, take your meds (and have a regime for doing so since you won't be able to rely on your home habits).

It's a good idea to think about vacations that cater especially to the needs of seniors—like special cruises or coach-based trips. That way, you avoid the intrusions of the noisier younger generation!

WATCH OUT FOR THESE TRAVEL SCAMS

When you're in unfamiliar territory, it's easy to get duped by tricksters who prey on vacationers. And remember, scams and scammers come in a variety of shapes, and sizes, although they're more common abroad than in the US. Here are the eight most common travel scams to watch out for:

1. **Currency Tricks**

   Change money at banks or well-known agents; skip the booths and traders who may offer poor exchange rates or add on unexpected charges.

   Watch out for sleight-of-hand trader-tricksters who switch the note you give them, then claim you haven't paid enough. Others just give you the wrong change. Check it!

2. **Panhandlers**

   Panhandlers hang out in the same places as tourists and usually have a moving tale of woe to tell. They are usually kids themselves or are accompanied by children. If they don't speak the language, they may hand you a note with a plea for help.

   If they're kids, they may belong to organized begging rings and see very little of the cash they collect.

3. **Phony Collectibles and Souvenirs**

   Buying memorabilia from your trip is part of the fun of travel, but don't be fooled into thinking you're getting a bargain. That rarely, if ever, happens, and most items, even if they look old and valuable, were probably made last week.

Buy something because you like it, not because it seems to have a good value. While you're at it, watch out for street solicitors inviting you to special events (jewelry and carpet factory tours, China tea ceremonies, and so on). They're on commission, and you could get cornered into paying a lot of money for questionable value.

4. Timeshare Lures

Don't get me wrong; people own and enjoy timeshares but pretty much every resort abroad that you visit these days has unscrupulous characters trying to lure you to a presentation with free gift offers or scratch cards that always "win." The catch is that you have to go with them to collect.

They try to hijack you at the airport, on the beach, or in a restaurant. They will tell you it's not a timeshare; it's a travel club or similar, and you can't go wrong. Resist the high pressure, and don't go to the presentation.

5. Discount Travel Cards

Discount travel cards are another high-pressure trick to run away from. Telesales and other solicitors will try to offer you a card they claim will earn big discounts on accommodation and other travel costs.

They may even offer incentives like free flights. Mostly the cards, which cost around $500 bucks—and the tickets—are worthless.

6. Bogus Front Desk Credit Card Checks

Here's one scenario: You receive a call at your hotel supposedly from the front desk. The "clerk," who is, in reality, a crook, phoned the hotel and asked for your room number. He says there's been a problem with your credit card and asks you to repeat the number along with the security code on the back.

If you get a call like this, just say you'll come down to the lobby to clear the issue up.

7. **Phony Tour Guides**

In some countries—India and Egypt, for example—locals hang out at historic sites, claiming to be official guides.

They will overcharge you and then give a half-hearted tour or make an excuse and disappear. Plan your tours and book guides in advance—or buy a book and self-guide yourself.

8. **Rental Car Cons**

Rental car cons come in all sorts of varieties. Most common is the loading of the basic rental fee with all kinds of phony or unnecessary extras, claiming the car is damaged when you return it and overcharging for refueling.

Make sure you know all the charges before you rent; scrutinize the auto when you collect it, pointing out any defects and photographing them if necessary, and return it full of fuel. Better yet, use one of the reputable auto rental agencies.

Some things you can do to cut the risk of being snared by a scammer include not dressing like a tourist, appearing confident rather than hesitant, being firm in your refusal to speak to a suspicious person or deal with them. To borrow a phrase: Just say "No!"

FINALLY ... SOME IMPORTANT INSURANCE ISSUES

When it comes to health insurance, you absolutely must check the terms of your health policy dealing with out-of-state and overseas coverage. Note that Medicare and Medicaid won't pay for care outside the US.

Second, check your homeowner's policy to establish if it covers things like loss of or damage to your personal belongings on vacation.

Third, with so many flights delayed or canceled through security or environmental issues (think Icelandic volcanoes) and with the possibility of a family issue forcing you to cancel, seriously consider travel insurance. Do note that some credit card providers offer insurance for travel paid for with their card. Check that out first.

CHAPTER SEVEN

CAN THE SPAM, BAM THE SCAMMERS

It's a sad fact of life that a small percentage of our population seems to think it's okay to take stuff from us that doesn't belong to them. What's worse, they often target the most vulnerable folk, like seniors or the unemployed, and they count on naivete to snare their victims.

We call some of these bad guys fraudsters, confidence tricksters, or scammers (although we might be tempted to use stronger language!), and they rob the American people of tens of billions of dollars every year. Sometimes they even rob people of their identity and livelihood.

A growing population of internet users has only added to our woes. The internet makes it easier for the crooks to target their victims and gives them a whole arsenal of weapons with which to attack. But they shouldn't be able to get away with it.

For a start, there's a whole array of government and other agencies dedicated to fighting back, including the Federal Trade Commission (FTC), the Internet Crime Complaint Center (part of the FBI), and the Better Business Bureau.

In addition, there are hundreds of anti-scam information websites. Then, of course, there's the internet security software we're supposed to have on our computers that can stop scam artists dead in their tracks.

Yet, somehow, millions of us still fall for the cons. Allow me to explain the 10 most common types of scams, and what you can do to spot and avoid them—and what to do if you don't.

It goes without saying that there are obviously more than 10 categories of scams—since many of them overlap. No matter the category, they're all intended to do one thing – steal from you. Let's take a look.

TEN CATEGORIES OF SCAMS

1. Identity Theft

This is by far the most common scam, costing consumers and businesses billions a year. In simple terms, identity theft happens when someone gets information about you that enables them to pretend they are you.

Most often, they use this fraud to take money from your bank account, borrow money, or use your credit card to buy stuff—especially on the internet. But scammers have also been known to completely assume someone else's identity, so they can get a job or healthcare.

They may just steal your wallet or purse to get the info. But their basic weapon is a sort of "hook and line." They bait you by posing as an organization like your bank, the police, a utility company, a government department, or even your favorite internet shopping site, and then they request personal information like account details, passwords, and social security numbers.

It's kind of like fishing, so it's called "phishing." Crooks usually phish online by getting you to visit a bogus page they've disguised to look like the real thing, such as Amazon or PayPal, for instance. Then they ask you to sign on. Or they may send you a message by email, text, or make a phone call to you, often claiming to be from your bank and warning you that your account has been blocked. They may ask you to call a 1-800 number where, again, they will ask for your account details.

Another sneaky trick for computer users causes a warning message to flash up on-screen, suggesting that your PC is infected with a virus and inviting you to download a program to deal with it. In fact, this program actually downloads "spyware" that checks your computer for confidential information, like account numbers and passwords. Once it gathers your data, it sends it back to the scammer.

Crooks also plant spyware on your computer by sending emails with attachments or links to other websites that they ask you to click.

There are far too many ruses used by identity thieves to list here, but you can learn a lot more about this crime from the FTC.

However, there are a number of things you can do to minimize the chances of getting scammed, including:

This is why you want to install internet security software on your PC and keep it up to date. These programs will spot spoof websites. You can pay up to $70 for this protection, but there are good free programs like Microsoft's Security Essentials or the free antivirus program from Avast Antivirus.

Never take someone's word that they are who they say they are without absolute proof.

If you're asked to call your bank or credit card company or visit their website, never use the contact details in the message. Key in the number or email address from your contacts list or phone book.

Don't open attachments or click on links in emails from people you don't know—especially if they seem sensational or worrying (like they claim to have weird photos of you).

Use passwords that contain a mixture of numbers and letters, with a different password for each account. Even if it's inconvenient, change them regularly. Never tell anyone your passwords, and don't store them in an easily accessible place.

Monitor and check all your financial statements regularly, so you can quickly spot any spending that's not yours.

Similarly, monitor your status with the credit reporting agencies to see if someone has applied for a loan or created a debt in your name.

You're entitled to one free report from each of the three agencies per year.

If you suspect you are the victim of identity theft, report it to the police straightaway, close any accounts you think may have been compromised, and notify the credit reporting agencies.

Unfortunately, sorting things out once you have been stung in this way can be a time-consuming process, but the FTC provides a no-nonsense checklist, complete with forms and templates.

2. Home Scams

How often does someone knock at your front door trying to sell you something or attempting to raise money for charity? Fairly regularly, I would guess—unless you happen to live in the middle of nowhere!

But, as I pointed out in the previous section: How do you know they're who they say they are? Even if they have what appears to be an ID card or a truck with a logo, these things are easily forged.

Once again, being skeptical is my number one Rule—even if it means running the risk of shutting the door in the face of someone who's really genuine.

What I call doorstep scammers come in a variety of guises. For example, there are bogus contractors who either tell you there's something wrong with your house, or they might offer to do roofing or paving maintenance.

Engage them, and they'll overcharge, do a bad job, or simply take your money and run.

Then there are phony utility workers who claim they need to check something. These creeps either come inside and steal from you or get you outside while an accomplice goes inside and does the same thing.

Others may ask for information as a prelude to identity theft or claim to be raising money for a local charitable cause or the police or fire service.

There's a simple rule for dealing with these people, whether they're frauds or not—don't deal with them! If you need a contractor, whether it's a gardening service or roof repair expert, use the phone book or, better yet, recommendations from friends and relatives.

Make it a rule to always check a business' license with your local city or county government, and learn about their track record with your local Better Business Bureau.

If you want to give money to a charity, take the details from the solicitor, then check it out. Only when you are assured the organization is legitimate then send your money directly to the charity.

If a utility worker turns up unannounced on your doorstep, send them away while you check with the utility company.

Be equally wary if you get a phone call supposedly from the company trying to make an appointment. Ask for the caller's name and number, then look the real number up in the phone book and ask for the named individual.

In addition, never give confidential information or money to someone you don't know. Don't be taken in by sob stories—like students selling magazine subscriptions or artwork to help pay for college (a common trick)—and don't allow a stranger over your threshold.

If they say they need to make an emergency call, let them use your cell phone outside (and if you don't have a cell, politely say you can't help or, if you think it's a real emergency, shut your door and dial 911 yourself).

3. Spam and Bogus Offers

We used to call it junk mail in the old days, but in the internet era, it's referred to as "spam." It's all the same thing: Unsolicited offers to sell you something that, at best, you don't want, and at worst, doesn't even exist.

Spam still arrives in your "snail mail" (via the USPS), in your email inbox, or even via those infuriating telesales reps who always seem to call just as you're sitting down for dinner.

Of course, not every solicitation is a scam, but a high proportion of them are—especially offers for health products and financial services.

Spam largely consists of fake people and companies making dubious claims about what they can do for you and, if you fall for their persuasive or high-pressure sales techniques, you can end up giving them the very information I warned about divulging when we discussed identity theft. In some cases, you may simply pay for a product or service that doesn't work.

These sharks may tell you to act fast, or the deal will be gone, or they may offer you what sounds like a fantastic prize like free air tickets. Believe me; you either won't get them, they'll be expensive or will have difficult strings attached.

The old adage works best here" "If it sounds too good to be true, it probably is."

Here are a few more tips you can use to can the spammers:

- Register with the Do Not Call Registry to stop telemarketers.

- Unfortunately, there's no do-not-spam list, but you can set up a spam filter for your email.

- Never respond to a spam message, no matter how enticing. Once you do, your name will go onto what crooks call a "sucker list." You don't need me to tell you what that is.

- Beware of bogus online pharmacies selling cheap meds without a prescription. They only want your money or will sell drugs of uncertain quality.

  This doesn't include genuine online pharmacies that will be properly registered with state or federal agencies and will require a prescription.

One final thought....

Do you get the emails that ask you to pass them on to 10 other people, or something awful will happen? Here's my advice: Don't, and it won't. If you do, you're just adding to the spam avalanche.

4. Advance Payment Fraud

This is sometimes known as the Nigerian 419 fraud (named for the article in Nigerian legislation which deals with this crime). Nigeria, and at least several African states, is mostly where this con comes from.

Often this crime originates as a form of spam, which, if you use email, you will almost certainly have received. It's a message inviting you to help someone get millions of dollars out of the country, for which you will be handsomely rewarded.

Or maybe they'll tell you they've tracked you down and have a large inheritance waiting for you. If you fall for it, sooner or later, you'll get a message asking for money to help move the cash before they can get it to you—that's the advance payment and where they get you.

In one variation, you get a message saying you've won a lottery fortune. Again, you'll be asked to pay taxes or administration fees before you get your money.

Other well-known advance payment frauds involve sending out a check to victims—this could be for anything from a house rental payment to supposedly funding a "secret shopping" assignment—in which you're asked to remit part of the money you get to a third party.

After you do this, the original check you banked is found to be a forgery, and you're out the amount you forwarded to the third party, i.e., the scammer.

All these advance payment scams have one thing in common; they ask you to send money using one of the legitimate electronic cash wiring services.

Such payments are often impossible to trace, and of course, it puts your cash instantly into the hands of the crook, well before you find the check you got was a dud. There are two simple rules to remember here: Never forward part of a check payment from someone you don't know, and never send wire payments to strangers.

5. Investment Scams

It used to be that only rich people put big money into investments. However, these days, most of us have our futures tied up in IRAs, 401ks, and money market accounts.

It's bad enough that these accounts can be subject to the turbulence of stock market performance or interest rate see-saws, but you could be doing a whole lot worse with your money, like watching it disappear into the bottomless pit of a scammer's pocket.

The notorious case of Bernie Madoff is just one, albeit the biggest, instance of Ponzi investment schemes—named for the originator of this fraud in which victims invest large sums of money on the promise of big returns.

The Ponzi scheme relies on more and more people joining because their money is used to pay earlier investors—after the scammer has skimmed off his take. When the scheme runs out of investors, as it did with Madoff, it collapses, and most of the money is found to have disappeared.

Other common investment cons include what is called "pump and dump" schemes, in which the crook spreads false stories about the success prospects of a company where he owns stock. Investors buy the stock, the price rises, and the scammer dumps his shares at this higher level before the price collapses again.

Yet other scams lure people into investing in projects. Energy schemes are a favorite. The promoter may claim that this project will be the next big thing. Often the product or service is heavily overrated, under-developed, or non-existent.

Investment scammers are sneaky, too. Frequently, they worm their way into social groups, like churches and community organizations, where they make friends, build up the trust of members, then pounce.

Again there are just a couple of simple rules that will keep you clear of these fraudsters:

If you're promised a higher than average rate of return, know that it's either a scam or an unacceptably high risk.

Always discuss planned investments with your stockbroker or other trusted financial advisor.

A hot investment tip from a friend should be treated the same way as if it came from a total stranger—with lots of skepticism!

6. Other Financial Scams

The recession of 2008/2009 left many people struggling to keep their heads above water, financially speaking. Since recovery takes years rather than months, the struggle likely will continue for some time.

But other people's financial misfortunes are a golden opportunity for scammers.

Their tricks include foreclosure rescue scams in which victims pay a hefty fee believing the scammer will save their homes for them, only for these criminals to never be seen again; remortgage and reverse mortgage deals which can lose homeowners a small fortune and even their home; and bogus personal and business loans that either require an arrangement fee or charge unbelievably high levels of interest.

Then there's a whole bunch of credit cards scams. You know the sort where you're told that no matter how bad your credit is, you qualify for a card.

Usually, you have to call a 900 premium charge number for the details (cha-ching!), then pay a fee dressed up as some sort of administration charge (cha-ching!), and then maybe you'll get a card that charges an annual fee and exorbitant rates (cha-ching, cha-ching!). Or maybe, for your money, the scammer will just send you a list of banks currently offering credit cards.

Crooks exploit the fact that people in financial difficulties don't like to talk about their problems. They take advantage of those in financial need being desperate to get things straight without others finding out. The truth is that the best way to deal with pressing financial problems is to talk to your bank or other lender.

Think twice before paying someone who promises they can solve your financial problems.

7. Job Scams

Another unsavory side to an economic downturn is the rise in unemployment and in the number of tricksters making money by claiming they can help people find jobs.

At its simplest, this con trick simply involves charging a fee for a non-existent job or for a list of publicly notified vacancies.

Sometimes, this is used as a cover for identity theft when the recruiter asks victims to provide confidential information, such as their social security number. They ask for this to supposedly run a verification check.

Or they may ask you to pay for a credit check or even direct you to a bogus site (which they own and operate) where, again, you must pay for a credit check.

In the last few years, there's also been a surge in the number of people working from home and a corresponding rise in work-from-home scams.

Many of these cons are based on genuine job ideas—like medical bill processing or home word processing—but the scams are usually covers for nothing more than selling a list of firms that do use work-from-home or other questionable training courses that will supposedly give you the skills you need.

If you're looking for employment, whether in a normal work environment or at home, bear these safety guidelines in mind:

- If you're asked to pay to get a job, even if it's a fee for a verification process, it's highly likely to be some sort of scam.

- For every legitimate work-from-home job, there are hundreds of potential applicants and potential scams. The odds of landing the real deal are low.

- Be wary about giving any confidential information before you actually start work.

8. Online Sales

The number of incidents where people paid for goods they didn't receive through auction sites like eBay and classified ad sites like Craigslist is alarming, though both organizations and many others have taken big steps to cut down on this crime.

So, crooks have turned to a new trick: setting up whole websites selling a wide range of non-existent products. These sites are well-designed and often have credit card signs and other logos that make them seem real.

The really bad side of these sites is that they take not only your money, but your credit card details that can then be used for identity theft.

Buying and paying for stuff you've never seen from someone you don't know has to be considered risky but you're less vulnerable if you use a credit card or PayPal, which provides a degree of cover against fraud.

On auction and other used product internet sites, a seller's track record will also help you judge their reliability, while on classified sites, it's better if you can buy locally, where you can inspect the product before paying for it.

As for bogus websites, you can't do a great deal other than steer clear of trading names you don't know. Some internet security software, when integrated with your web browser, will also highlight suspicious sites.

9. "Send Money" Pleas

If you're one of those people who feel moved to give money to panhandlers, maybe you part with a dollar bill or two. But victims of online money pleas often end up paying a heck of a lot more. This scam takes two main forms:

1. A message, via email or one of the social networks like Facebook, seeming to come from someone you know, claims they're stranded in a foreign country. They ask you to send money to get them out of a fix. In reality, a scammer has hijacked that person's email or other account and is sending the note to all their listed contacts.

2. The "grandparent scam." – Seniors receive a call that starts with "Hello Grandma/Grandpa." The caller (a scammer) hopes the person will say something like: "Is that you, Billy (or another name)?" so he can confirm this, and then go ahead and spin a story about being in a fix in another country (usually Canada) and needing money urgently.

As with the advance payment scam outlined above, both tricks rely on you using an untraceable money wire to send the cash. If you receive either of these messages, they're almost certainly scams. But if you're unsure, check out the story with other friends and relatives who should know the whereabouts of the supposed caller.

10. The Best (or Worst) of the Rest

This is my catch-all bullet point because, of course, there are literally hundreds of other scams out there. I already listed some of the cons you might encounter on vacation, but here are a few others to be aware of:

- ATM tricks. These might include phony fronts that crooks attach to an ATM to read the details on your card or devices they insert in the slot to prevent your card from being returned. Inspect the ATM closely, and if you lose your card this way, contact your bank immediately.

- Parking lot encounters. These include people selling stuff out the back of a truck (often in genuine product boxes they've stuffed with junk) or others selling supposed precious metal or stones. In reality, these people are working with an accomplice who vouches for their value. Just don't buy.

- Auto Repairs - These range from tricksters who stop you in a parking lot, tell you there's smoke coming from your car, and offer to fix it—for a price—and unscrupulous auto repair shops who use cheap parts or exaggerate the work that needs to be done. Always get your auto checked only by a reputable dealer.

- Forged tickets for big sports and entertainment events. Buy your tickets from recognized sources, or don't buy at all. Adhere to this rule, especially if the event involves expensive travel (like the Olympics, which in 2008, cost victims many millions of dollars).

- Animal scams, like forged certificates for supposed pedigree pets, illegal sale of rare or exotic creatures, or shady characters who collect your pet after you advertise that you're giving it way, then mistreat it or put it up for sale.

FINALLY....

Well, I could go on at length about this evil crime because there are very few people who don't encounter a scam attempt at some time in their lives.

Unfortunately, scammers are not stupid. They're often very clever, plausible people who know how to spin a convincing story. What's more, new scams appear almost by the day, so it's easy to be caught unawares.

But avoiding a scam so often comes down to commonsense, keeping tabs on the latest tricks, and administering a powerful dose of healthy skepticism!

If you suspect you've been scammed, always tell the police. Too many people are embarrassed to admit this, but by reporting the incident, there's a chance you may recover your money or, at the very least, prevent someone else from being caught out by the same trick.

I also encourage you to make time to visit the FTC website or contact them for a list of available publications. The better informed you are, the more likely you are to avoid a scam!

CHAPTER EIGHT

KEY STEPS TO ENSURE YOUR HEALTH & FITNESS

What do fitness and good health mean to you? To me, they mean making the most of your body's potential for wellness.

We don't all start from the same position when it comes to getting fit or being healthy. One of the features of humanity is that we're all different.

Because of inherited factors, disease, or disability, some of us are less physically able to perform certain tasks than others. This means that portion of the population has to try a bit harder to achieve the same level of well-being that others may reach with ease.

That's why when you embark on any serious fitness and health program, you should seek professional advice from your doctor and perhaps a coach at your local gym or a dietician.

Having said that, let's have a show of hands from everyone who believes they really do make the most of their body's potential for wellness.

Uh-oh.

Just as I thought, not many of you.

In fact, to some extent, even serious athletes and super-fit people occasionally fall short of their own high standards.

As for me, I'm a repeat offender! It's human nature, so there's no need to feel too guilty about it.

Instead, let's just paint a picture of what a fit and healthy you might look like. We'll include some tips on special health issues like allergies while always bearing in mind the point I just made about everyone being different – and, accordingly, understanding that we may have different health goals and measures of success.

We're going to do this by looking at the key components of physical well-being: weight, diet, exercise, blood pressure and blood count, and medicines.

Of course, you're unlikely to be at a healthy weight if you don't follow an appropriate diet and exercise program, for instance. Still, I'm not going to claim that I have all the answers. I'm not a professional health advisor, and the information I give here is purely for educational purposes, not for the diagnosis or treatment of any conditions. Although, I do want to provide you with food for thought (pardon the pun) that might help make a difference to your wellness. At the end of the day, only you can take the right steps to get you there.

(By the way, I'm talking about general wellness and won't be discussing certain critical health issues like substance abuse or specific disorders, like diabetes, for instance, here. They're beyond the capacity of this book.)

The great thing about trying to improve your health and fitness is that there are so many resources that offer support. In particular, a national initiative aims to improve people's lives, prevent, and reduce the costs of disease, and promote community health and wellness.

YOUR BODY MASS INDEX – A WEIGHTY ISSUE

I remember once having to get weighed in public because I was about to travel in a seaplane where total weight aboard the craft is a critical issue.

My weight was okay, but there was a heavier lady in our group, and the process, unfortunately, involved the weight-checker yelling the numbers to a colleague who was tallying the total.

I don't remember what this poor woman weighed, but I will never forget how uncomfortable she looked when the announcement was made. It reminds me that although none of us wants to be too heavy (okay, maybe a few eccentrics do), most of us struggle all our adult lives with the challenge of controlling our weight.

There's no doubt that some people tend to put on weight easier than others. That's down to the way our bodies metabolize (burn up and convert) the food we eat. We spread that weight around to different parts of the body, men to the abdomen, and women to the hips and thighs, for instance.

That extra stuff is critical to our good health because it's not your actual weight that counts in the fitness stakes but the ratio of weight to height.

Remember when the rule of thumb was that if you could "pinch an inch," you probably had too much fat. Now we go by something more scientific that we call Body Mass Index or BMI.

You calculate this by:

1. Multiplying your weight in pounds by 703,
    (e.g., 150 x 703 = 105,450);

2. Multiplying your height in inches by itself
    (e.g. 66 x 66 = 4,356); and

3. Dividing the first number by the second
    (e.g., 105,450/4356 = 24.2, your BMI)

In fact, if you have internet access, you can go online to do the math for you.

If your BMI is above 25 (like it is for one-third of all Americans), you've got work to do.

Sorry if that was painful for you. But here's the really bad news. According to the Weight-control Information Network, which is part of the US Department of Health, if you are among that one-third, you may be at greater risk of suffering: Type 2 diabetes, coronary heart disease, and stroke, metabolic syndrome, certain types of cancer, sleep apnea, osteo-arthritis, gallbladder disease, fatty liver disease, or pregnancy complications.

Now, let's look at some of the potential solutions.

YOUR BON APPÉTIT DIET

I don't know about you, but I've lost count of the number of different fad diets I've tried. Some work, some don't, but most of them don't last because they become boring at some point or exclude a favorite food you just can't live without.

So, although I don't have an earth-shattering secret to successful diet-ing, I have learned it has a lot to do with two things: Respect for your body and a good helping of willpower.

Let's examine the components of a healthy diet, as defined by the US Department of Agriculture. They call this arrangement a food pyramid, but it's fair to say that over the years, they've moved away from the strict idea of a broad base representing the things we should eat most of and a tiny top for what we should eat the least of.

The USDA says a healthy diet:

1. Emphasizes fruits, vegetables, whole grains, and fat-free or low-fat milk and milk products.

2. Includes lean meats, poultry, fish, beans, eggs, and nuts.

3. Is low in saturated fats, trans fats, cholesterol, salt (sodium), and added sugars.

4. Other diets, as you probably know, put more emphasis on reduced carbohydrate or higher protein intake while yet more focus on a single type of food (like grapefruit or cabbage).

   Opinion on their long-term effectiveness is divided, but what we do know is that weight gain is a direct result of taking in more calories than your body needs. So, one way or another, a weight loss program only works if you reduce your caloric intake.

One of the reasons why low carb diets seem effective is because they're more filling, thereby reducing the number of calories you actually eat. Whether this approach is healthy in the long term, I'm not qualified to say!

Good dietary health is not only about being the correct weight. You also need a balanced diet that supplies vitamins (like thiamin and niacin, as well as those with letters), minerals (iron, zinc, etc.), and other nutrients your body needs, which is what the food pyramid sets out to do.

For example, strawberries, which also happen to be wonderfully tasty fruits, are considered nutrient-dense, with lots of fiber and Vitamin C. Blueberries also rate highly in this area, as do vegetables like broccoli and cauliflower.

On the other hand, many foods, especially processed types, lack nutrients and may be high in sugar. Our bodies need *some* sugar—but not in the quantities most of us consume!

But how in the world do we stick to a healthy diet? As I said, many people fail on this mission, so it's worth noting the following tips, some of which come from the non-profit organization helpguide.org:

1. Take your time planning and implementing your diet. It's best to introduce small changes gradually rather than tackling them in one big swipe. Don't set unrealistic targets for your weight loss.

2. Also, take your time eating your food. Part of the joy of eating is the taste, not just the desire to feel full. Chew your food slowly, thoughtfully. Experience the taste!

3. Plan your meals well in advance. As LaGuardia.edu says: "You will have won half the healthy diet battle if you have a well-stocked kitchen, a stash of quick and easy recipes, and plenty of healthy snacks."

4. Cut down on the size of your portions, rather than forcing yourself to eliminate the foods you really love. If you reduce the size, you can eat more frequently, which also helps to stave off hunger and craving. But when you do feel the urge to eat, think about whether you're truly hungry or just craving the taste.

5. Have plenty of variety on your plate, especially colorful foods, like veggies and fruits. Psychologically, they make for a more interesting and satisfying meal.

6. If you can, team up with your partner or a friend to support each other and share recipes (and even meals!)

7. Don't give up! Everyone goes off the rails now and then by over-indulging at the ice cream parlor or something similar. Never let your inner-critic suggest that's the end of your sensible diet. Just start over.

THE PERFECT HEALTH PARTNERSHIP

You can do all the dieting in the world, and you may even lose weight, but you won't be a whole lot fitter unless you combine it with a sensible exercise regime—again under the guidance of a professional.

In fact, diet and exercise are the perfect health partnership. Each supports the other. As with diet, everyone's needs and capabilities differ, so you need to develop a personal fitness program tailored to yours.

A couple of years back, the US Department of Health issued its Physical Activity Guidelines for Americans, with a theme underlining the individual nature of exercise programs: "Be Active Your Way."

Its key recommendations for adults include:

1. Doing at least 10 minutes of physical activity at a time, mixing both aerobic activities (exercises that make you breathe harder) with muscle strengthening (push-ups, sit-ups, or weight-lifting, for example).

2. Increasing the time and effort you put in as you get fitter and exercising this way, ideally at least three days a week.

3. Moderate exercise should total at least two-and-a-half hours a week, while vigorous workouts should be at least one-and-a-quarter.

4. Moderate exercise equates to activity that pushes your breathing effort slightly; as the experts put it: You're able to talk but not sing. Examples include yard work, dancing, walking briskly, and even washing the car.

5. Vigorous exercise really gets your breathing going so that you can only say a few words before gasping. You'd be doing this with more active dancing (like an aerobics class), cycling reasonably fast, jogging, or uphill walking, doing martial arts, or swimming fast.

6. However, if all this seems too much for you right now, feel free to start at a much easier level by doing things like standing instead of sitting to perform certain chores, playing a musical instrument (also good for strengthening your breathing if you choose a wind instrument), cooking (watch those calories, though!) or other household or garage tasks.

7. The key to success is to do what you enjoy – walking, for instance, is popular, easy for all age groups, and can be adjusted to suit an individual's age and abilities. Exercise classes can also be fun because they have the social element of working out together and sharing in the effort.

8. If you exercise in groups or alone to the sound of music, find tunes you really enjoy and that motivate you to push just a little harder.

   But don't push too hard. If you experience any kind of pain or dizziness while you're exercising, stop and, if necessary, get medical help. Here are a few other tips for safe exercising.

9. Always do a few minutes of stretching exercises to warm up before you start.

10. Keep yourself well-hydrated, and drink plenty of water before, during, and after your workout.

11. If you're outside, protect yourself from the weather by using sunscreen or wearing layers of clothing that you can remove as you heat up.

12. Wear the right gear for the task. It pays to invest in good sports shoes, which reduce pressure on the feet and legs, for instance. Make sure you also wear protective gear for cycling or hiking.

Are you up for this? Need some help? There's a great Government program called the President's Challenge, which encourages all American's to be active every day. The program is split into age groups: younger kids, teens, adults, and seniors, and offers a series of challenges, an awards scheme, and some useful tools to help.

I especially like the campaign's "Ten Ideas To Get Active," which underlines how simple tasks, like walking the dog, mowing the lawn, or parking a distance from and walking to your destination, can make a big difference.

MONITORING YOUR HEALTH

I know people who haven't visited a doctor in 20 years. Obviously, they're in good health, but I do question the wisdom of not keeping track of what's going on inside their bodies as they get older.

I'm not one for buying up those mobile package deals you get flyers about, where they do everything except measure your toenails, but I do recommend regular preventive screenings for key health issues like mammograms and pap smears, colonoscopies, and prostate testing, plus an annual physical check-up, including blood work, especially once you reach middle age.

If you have a family history of particular types of disease, always discuss with your doctor how soon and how often you should be tested.

The reason for all these precautions is simple: Many of the serious illnesses we suffer later in life are the cumulative effect of disorders we could have identified and dealt with when they were relatively minor.

The key health indicators you might want to watch (plus others advised by your physician) includes blood pressure, blood count, glucose levels, cholesterol, liver function, and cardiovascular sensitivity.

There are also a number of things you can do to actively monitor your own health. Nobody knows your body better than you do, and while I wouldn't want to encourage you to become a hypochondriac, I also advise you against ignoring the signals that all is not well from your body.

Pay close attention to persistent headaches, sleeplessness, poor digestive function, chest pain, severe memory loss, and prolonged, severe joint or muscular pain.

As you get older, it's a good idea too to check your blood pressure regularly. These days, you can buy reliable home testing equipment for under $100. Some of these machines also monitor your pulse and detect an irregular heartbeat.

Also, always keep a record of your readings as they do vary from one moment to the next, and only a consistent record can show you how you're really doing.

FOOD ALLERGIES

Scientists and nutrition experts increasingly recognize that certain foods that most of us enjoy can have a disastrous effect on the lives of others. Sometimes it's so bad that eating the wrong food can spark an allergic reaction that can close the throat (anaphylaxis).

Other times a reaction to a specific food may be categorized as an intolerance. The effect may not be as severe, but it can cause distress and discomfort, especially over a prolonged period. A whole swath of food categories can be included, such as dairy products (lactose intolerance), fructose (an ingredient of sugar and natural substance in fruits), gluten (from wheat), yeast, caffeinated drinks, and individual produce items like peanuts and certain fruits.

Often, the link between a food and the reactions are not immediately identified, causing the victim to suffer for years, but it's now possible to use fairly reliable tests—at special allergy clinics or from a gastroenterologist.

You can also monitor your own bodily reactions to food by varying your diet over a period of time and keeping a record of the result. Eating chocolate, for example, gives some people headaches. Isn't that bad luck!

If you suspect a food intolerance, you might try an elimination diet, in which you remove whole categories of food for several weeks and again keep records as to how you are affected.

A word of caution: This, and the more severe version where you start with a very basic food, then add in others gradually, should only be undertaken with professional guidance.

TAKING MEDICATIONS

I want to talk about four important points here:

1. **Remembering to take your meds:**

   It's so easy to forget to take your medicine. Save yourself some trouble and worry, and try some of these tips from the National Heart, Lung, and Blood Institute:

   ❑ Take them at the same time every day and try to link them with something else you do routinely, like brushing your teeth.

   ❑ Write a reminder on a sticky note and leave it on your bathroom mirror. Change the position and even the color of the note regularly, so you don't get used to it.

   ❑ Keep a chart that records when you took your meds. Use color coding, so you know what you took when.

❏ Use a pillbox with compartments marked with the days of the week.

❏ Ask friends and family to help with reminders, and even set up your computer to give you a nudge.

2. **Identifying drug side effects and interactions:**

A friend of mine who was put on a cholesterol-lowering medication happened to love a glass of grapefruit juice with his breakfast every day. It seemed healthy enough until one week later; he spotted a yellow warning on the pill bottle: "Avoid large amounts of grapefruit juice." Yikes!

Fortunately, he didn't suffer any side effects, but his story underlines the importance of reading medication instructions carefully and making the time to read any small print about side effects. You'll see this inform-ation in magazine ads, online, and in printed matter that comes with your prescription. It's tedious reading, I know, but potentially life-saving!

In addition to not mixing grapefruit juice with certain pills, there's a whole science of how drugs interact with each other. If you're taking more than one prescribed medicine, check to learn about the interac-tions with your pharmacist.

3. **Using over-the-counter products**

It's a common mistake to think that just because you don't need a prescription to buy certain pharmaceutical products, they must be safe to use. Not so.

Over-the-counter (OTC) meds can also have interaction problems, as outlined above, and many can have serious consequences if overdosed.

Once again, ensure that you read the labels and other literature care-fully. If in doubt, talk to a pharmacist.

4. Vitamins and health food products

There's a big debate about just how good vitamin supplements and other health foods really are for you. Personally, I take a daily vitamin supplement and fish oil.

Every so often, I see reports that say something we once believed to be good for us turns out to have no beneficial effect. It also seems you can have too much of a good thing, as is the case with overdoses of certain vitamins or minerals.

Then just as we start to get used to one regimen, suddenly, there's a new fad—a drink that's supposed to have wondrous health properties or a pill that can help us lose weight. As I mentioned in the diet section, the best way to acquire vital nutrients is through a balanced diet, especially with plenty of varied vegetables.

HELPING OTHERS IMPROVE THEIR HEALTH

So far, maybe it seems like I've been talking directly to you about how to improve your health and fitness. But of course, everything I've suggested here can equally apply to your family and friends. Yet, if you think it's tough motivating yourself to get onto a healthier regimen, it can be twice the challenge to apply it to others, especially kids.

The best starting point is setting an example. People notice when you lose weight, become more vibrant and energetic, and often will comment on it, giving you the opportunity to encourage them to follow in your footsteps.

Children are less likely to respond to this kind of motivation, but it's still important that you set an example rather than employing the "Don't do as I do; do as I say" approach!

And while this is a sensitive topic, we do need to tell people they're overweight. They already know that, of course, so it may feel reasonable to discuss the issue with a loved one.

A better approach is to suggest taking up some kind of regular physical activity together, to prepare healthier meals, and make wellness a topic for discussion. As you explain your ideas, make it clear that you want to do this for yourself as well and that you hope the other person will support you (because, in fact, you, too, will benefit from the exercise.)

A simple approach is to invite them to go for a walk with you. This can start out as a stroll, but you can gradually speed up. Give encouragement to the other person, even for modest effort, and, if you're walking with a child, consider a simple reward (not food!).

In fact, you might also think of buying a birthday or Christmas gift (even a spur-of-the-moment one) that has a fitness theme, such as workout clothes or even a basketball or exercise ball (depending on who the recipient is).

The health and fitness of loved ones are arguably as important as your own well-being, so please do what you can to help them.

LASTLY...

If you have a roof over your head and food in the larder, there's nothing more important to your well-being than having health insurance.

Increasingly, companies are shifting the cost burden of medical cover onto employees. In a recession, more people who have lost their jobs have to insure themselves. Keep in mind, too, that implementation of a new health reform legislation can make it a legal requirement to have coverage. No matter what, just be prepared.

CHAPTER NINE

BUYING SECURITY AND PEACE OF MIND

"I know nothing about racing, and any money I put on a horse
is a sort of insurance policy to prevent it winning."
— *Frank Richardson*

I know what Frank means. You take out an insurance policy; you pay your premiums, and usually, you get nothing back. At least, that's how it seems. Of course, you get a fantastic return from your insurance premiums.

It may not always be easily quantifiable; indeed you hope it isn't, but having insurance is the greatest form of protection you can get. It creates total peace of mind, with the assurance that if things do go wrong, someone will be there to pick up the tab.

In fact, insurance is such a powerful and effective way of protecting your interests that people have been doing it for 5000 years—starting with Chinese traders who used to spread their risk of losing goods by putting them on a variety of different ships.

The Babylonians did a similar thing in about 1000 BC. Then we fast forward to genuine shipping insurance policies first negotiated in a London pub called Lloyd's (hence "Lloyds of London"), the founding of the first true insurance company in the wake of the Great Fire of London in the 17th Century, and finally the establishment of the first insurance company in the US, in South Carolina, in 1732.

How we insure ourselves has come a long way since those early days, but the principles of insurance remain the same. People pool their money together, knowing that only a few of them will suffer a disaster, so there'll be enough money in the pool to cover the cost of the mishaps.

Only, these days, the pool is managed by an insurance company that estimates the number of contributors who are likely to need a payout and therefore, the total amount needed. Dividing that by the number of policyholders produces the cost of an individual's contribution or premium.

The policy you get is a legal document that specifies the risks it covers and the terms and conditions under which it pays out—usually arising from an accident, mistake, or something unforeseen. Insurance is, in the words of the *Concise Encyclopedia of Economics*, "a stodgy domain," but you ignore it at your peril.

10 VITAL BENEFITS OF INSURANCE

The days when a few sea traders were the only people who needed to protect their interests are long gone. Most of us live in a fast-spinning world laden with financial and security risks, which, if we don't take steps to eliminate, could cost us our livelihoods, homes, cars, other possessions, and indeed, our lives. This is what having the right insurance can do for you:

1. You reduce or eliminate the risk of facing sudden, major expenses if you, your family, or your property suffer a misfortune.

2. You have the funds to meet the costs of any liability claims made against you when you get blamed for someone else's misfortune.

3. You create security for yourself and your family in the event that you lose your earning power through job loss or disability.

4. You provide financial security for your family in the event of your death.

5. You are covered if someone else who isn't injures you or damages your property.

6. You have the best chance of quickly recovering your lifestyle after damage to your property, with someone taking care of you while restoration or replacement is underway.

7. You improve your creditworthiness by being recognized as a responsible citizen and may even be able to raise funds on the security of a policy.

8. If you're in business, you can insure against risks that otherwise might not allow you to compete against bigger, financially stronger contenders.

9. You can protect yourself against the damage caused by some of the modern financial crimes, which are otherwise difficult for you to understand and assess—like identity theft.

10. By contributing to insurance companies, you are sharing in the cost of researching ways to improve our lives, making them safer and reducing risks.

Notice I said above, just before point #1: "having the right insurance." Just as our lives have become more complex, so has the insurance market. Without professional guidance, it's easy to end up with coverage that doesn't meet your needs. Meaning you can have too little, too much, or even the wrong type.

WHAT KIND OF INSURANCE DO YOU NEED?

This is one of those "well, it all depends" questions. Factors that might influence your insurance needs include your age or life stage, your gender, your family circumstances, where you live, what kind of job you have, your state of health (and family history of health issues), and a whole lot of other individual facts that add up to a simple conclusion:

Everyone's requirements are different, and almost certainly, you need someone to help you tailor an insurance program that not only meets your

present circumstances but also is flexible enough to adapt to the changes that probably lie ahead.

Now, let's examine the principal types of insurance and what they might mean for you:

LIFE INSURANCE

It's not pleasant to think about, but we all have a finite amount of time here, though most of us don't know what will happen and, therefore, how others will be affected when our time is up. Life insurance responds to that uncertainty by paying either a lump sum or a regular amount to our dependents or other beneficiaries.

There are two main types of life insurance. First, there's permanent life insurance, which is guaranteed to pay out whether you shuffle off this earth in one year or when you're past 100. You pay a premium that's fixed when you take out the policy in return for that assured payout. In a way, it's a partial form of saving, which will probably have a residual value if you decide to discontinue the policy.

The second type of life policy is known as term life insurance, which, as its name suggests, will pay out to your dependents if death occurs during an agreed-upon period—usually 10 to 15 years. After that, the policy lapses. Again, the premium is fixed for the term of the policy, but if you cancel it, there's probably no refund.

WHICH ONE IS RIGHT FOR YOU?

Because it does not pay if the policy expires before you do, term insurance premiums are cheaper, and the policy is well-suited for covering the expensive periods of your life, like when you're raising a family or paying a mortgage, for instance, especially if you are also on a tight budget.

On the other hand, you're not building up any savings, and when your term coverage expires, taking out a new policy will cost you substantially more than the previous one (because you'll be older).

With a permanent policy, your premium will always be the same, although higher than you would pay for a similar term policy. Your dependents will always have the comfort of knowing they will be provided for. Plus, as I said, because the benefit is guaranteed, your policy can be used as collateral for a loan.

When you take out life insurance, the insurer will generally require a medical examination as well as details of your health and that of your parents. This helps them calculate the risk they are covering.

In a few cases where the benefit is quite low or if the policy has a moratorium on paying out in the first couple of years, this requirement may be waived.

There could be circumstances when life insurance might be unnecessary for you. For instance, if you have significant savings, or at least sufficient funds to meet all the foreseeable needs of your dependents, you might not need it. Still, discuss this with your financial advisor.

In the meantime, a good start is to set out your current financial commitments and needs against any life coverage you may already have. This will give you an idea if there's a gap you need to fill.

HOMEOWNERS AND RENTERS

I can hardly imagine circumstances when you wouldn't want to have coverage for your home and personal possessions—either in the form of homeowners or renters insurance. Losing your home or personal possessions is traumatic enough—and some personal items are irreplaceable—without also having to worry about the financial consequences.

Even though there are many similarities between the two types of coverage, I'm going to discuss homeowners insurance first.

HOMEOWNER'S INSURANCE

A standard policy normally covers you for both damage to your property (structure and personal possessions) and any liability for injuries or damage that you, your family, or pets cause to others. It also provides funds for living expenses if you can't live in your home while it's being repaired or rebuilt after an insured incident.

Structural damage may be caused by fire or storm, and your policy should provide for full rebuilding costs. Many insurers have standard tables for calculating this, based on demolition, and building cost per square foot —and they will usually amend this automatically each year.

Note, however, that standard policies do not cover damage from earthquakes or natural flooding. Depending on the insurer, you can get separate "quake cover" or have it added to your existing policy.

Flood insurance is available through the National Flood Insurance Program and some private insurers, but you may need additional cover via your insurance agent for contents.

As a rough guide, coverage for possessions is generally around half the value of your structural coverage. But you may amend this if you think your personal items are worth significantly more or less.

It makes good sense to take a quick inventory of the value of your home contents. The policy covers you for damage or theft of items. It probably will have a limit on cover for valuable items, but it is possible to get additional coverage through an endorsement called Scheduled Personal Property.

Here are a few more tips and facts worth knowing when it comes to insuring your possessions:

1. You are normally covered for theft, loss, or damage to these items when you're away from home, too.

2. Keep a list of serial numbers for electronic items that might be stolen.

3. Taking photos of the contents of each room (and storing them away from the house) may be useful as a reminder or as proof of ownership in the event of a claim.

4. If you buy an expensive new item for the home, notify your insurer to add it to your policy, if necessary.

5. Coverage can equal the full, new, replacement cost, or it may be reduced to take account of the age of the lost or damaged item.

6. Renters insurance provides more or less the same kind of cover for your personal possessions and personal liability as outlined above, but because you don't insure the structure of the home (your landlord should do that), premiums are lower.

AUTOS AND OTHER VEHICLES

My chapter on road safety provides enough evidence of the need for auto insurance. Do remember that it's also a legal requirement under most circumstances.

It also happens to be the area of insurance that has the greatest variation in rates between individuals, not only because of key risk factors like age, type of vehicle, and where it's mainly used but also because it operates in an intensely competitive marketplace.

In addition, there are a number of important factors like the level of deductibles, credit score, driving and loss history, and even the amount of annual mileage that can significantly affect the rate.

A basic auto insurance policy provides you with cover against the following risks arising from an accident:

1. Injuries you (or the designated driver) cause to others, either when driving your own vehicle or driving someone else's with their permission.

2. Damage you cause to someone else's vehicle or property.

3. The cost of treatment for injuries to you or your passengers, and possibly other compensation, like lost earnings, for example.

4. Damage to your vehicle after a collision or other accidental incident (like a pothole). If the accident was not your fault, your insurer will try to recover their money from the other driver's insurer.

5. Theft of your auto or damage caused by something other than a collision with another vehicle—like a flood, hitting an animal, being hit by a falling object, or your engine catching fire.

6. The cost of towing and reimbursement for renting a replacement auto while yours is being repaired or replaced.

7. Uninsured drivers. If the accident is caused by an uninsured (or under-insured) driver, your policy will cover the cost of repairs and treatment. It may even cover you if you're a pedestrian injured in these circumstances.

8. Many states set minimum levels for coverage, especially for liability to other people, but if you feel this is inadequate for your circumstances, you can increase this. Individual policies also vary in terms

of the level of deductible permitted and payment for such events as windshield breakage.

9. In addition to regular auto insurance, you can also get policies specially tailored for the needs of motorcyclists (coverage is similar to that for autos) and RVers (cover varies depending on how the vehicle is used, e.g., as a permanent home). Talk to your insurance agent for more information and advice.

MEDICAL, DISABILITY, AND LONG-TERM CARE

Employers, even the big ones, are increasingly passing the cost of health insurance back to their employees, and, of course, many smaller firms or people employing part-timers simply choose not to provide these benefits at all. Then it's up to the individual to make their own arrangements.

This situation is likely to intensify in the coming years. Because of the shake-out caused by the recession, many more people are either unemployed or becoming self-employed and responsible for making their own insurance arrangements.

At the same time, at some points, legislation may require pretty much every individual to have coverage. One way or another, I expect to see a surge in the number of people contracting individually with medical insurers.

However, there are still a number of different options, depending on the level of cover you need (or can afford).

With an indemnity health plan, for instance, paying a monthly premium entitles you to visit any doctor or hospital and be reimbursed for the full cost of treatment, less any deductible or co-pay stipulated in the policy.

You can opt for an extremely high deductible if you like, depending on your plan—ranging from $5,000 or even $10,000 per year—which significantly cuts your premiums. This is sometimes known as catastrophic cover, meaning that full reimbursement is available once that high deductible has been exceeded.

A basic health plan is another lower-cost alternative, but it has quite a number of exclusions for items that aren't covered that you must pay for yourself.

A number of other plans fall into a category called managed care, but you may know them better as HMOs or PPOs.

With HMOs—Health Maintenance Organizations—you select a primary care physician from a provided list. They will look after your healthcare and make referral decisions for specialists. You can't go directly to a specialist without a referral. Again, you may have a deductible or co-pay.

With PPOs—Preferred Provider Organizations—you have more freedom to choose who you see for medical attention, but you may still be required to get referrals to a specialist for some conditions, and you will encounter different rates according to whether the doctor you see is a "preferred provider."

You may pay deductibles and co-pays, but individual consultation fees will tend to be lower because of discounts negotiated by your insurer.

There are a number of variations in the above policies, some of them dependent on state requirements. Other factors to consider regarding your medical insurance cover include:

1. Dental and optical services not being covered by standard health insurance. In this instance, you will need separate policies.

2. You can open and use a tax-sheltered Health Savings Account to meet your out-of-pocket medical expenses.

3. Injuries and treatment arising from auto accidents may be covered by your policies for these risks and those at home on your medical insurance, while injuries in the workplace can be covered by Workers Compensation insurance.

4. If you are retired or laid off, you can stay in your employers' group health insurance plan via what is known as COBRA. This is generally more costly than the rate your employer gets.

5. Age, low-income circumstances, and some types of disability may entitle you to subsidized health coverage via Medicare or Medicaid. Details are available from the Centers for Medicare and Medicaid Services. Some states also have their own similar plans.

6. Although it's a health-related issue, coverage for disability calls for a separate insurance policy. Its basic aim is to maintain a level of income in the event that you become temporarily or permanently unable to work.

7. If this situation arises from an injury sustained at work "on the job," you may be entitled to Workers Compensation. Your employer is also required (in most states) to provide coverage for short-term sick leave.

8. Longer-term illness or disability you suffer "off the job" is a different issue. Although larger firms may insure you against this, many do not, and you may then have to fall back on social security disability benefits and/or a disability insurance policy you bought yourself. These private policies can replace up to 60-70% of your income, tax-free (if you pay the premium yourself).

There are two types of policy: short-term (paying you for up to two years) and long-term (paying you for a specified period which can extend to an indefinite period). Both types have a waiting period during which no benefit is paid.

9. Long Term Care (LTC) insurance is another important dimension of your health care needs. As more of us (happily) are living longer, the need for specialist health care in later years that's not covered by Medicare is growing.

   Generally, LTC activates when a policyholder is unable to perform, without help, two or more of what are called Activities of Daily Living (ADLs). These include eating, bathing, toileting, getting in and out of bed or a chair, continence, and dressing.

   Depending on the policy, you may be covered for care in a nursing home, an assisted living facility or a day-care center. You may even be covered for at-home care. The cover may be for a specific or indefinite period.

   Whether and when you should take out an LTC policy is something you should discuss with your agent. One thing's for sure, if you don't have coverage and do need care; it is extremely expensive.

INSURANCE FOR BUSINESS

This section refers to insurance coverage for small businesses, although in many ways, it's not that different from the coverage a large organization would have.

If you're in business, you probably already have at the very least a Business Owners' Policy (BOP). But the changing nature of business, the economy, and the law means you should still keep this under regular review. If you're just about to go into business, a BOP is definitely your starting point.

Generally, it will cover your property (for similar risks to homeowners policies), disruption of the business caused by an accident or catastrophe, and liability for injuries or property damage you or your employees cause to others. In addition, you might want to consider separate insurance policies for:

1. Professional liability that covers you against financial losses suffered through legal actions brought against you.

2. A commercial auto insurance policy to cover any vehicles owned and operated by the company or for vehicles owned by individuals but used in the course of business.

3. Worker's Compensation insurance to provide medical care for employees injured at work. It may also cover you for any legal action taken against you by an injured employee. Some states also require employers to provide disability coverage.

4. Key Person Insurance. Small businesses often find themselves heavily dependent on the skills of one or more employees, whose death could significantly impact the viability of the business. In this case, you would take out a life insurance policy on these individuals. You pay the premium and are the beneficiary in the event of their death.

5. Commercial Umbrella Liability provides coverage beyond the basic liability insurance in your BOP and is especially useful when a liability claim involves litigation.

OTHER TYPES OF INSURANCE

These days, you can insure against almost any risk that would end up costing you money or causing a major inconvenience. That includes loss of employment (and issues related to it like mortgage repayments), travel insurance, veterinary medical insurance for your pet, and identity theft—to name just a few.

If you have any concerns about financial vulnerability, discuss these with your insurance agent.

SO, IS IT WORTH IT?

With so many risks to cover, most people have to prioritize and make concessions about what to insure and how much coverage to buy.

In fact, this can be such a challenge that the number one reason people cite for not having insurance when disaster strikes is that they were thinking about it or that they were planning to buy it, but they just never got around to it.

Don't hesitate when it's time to protect yourself. Here are some statistical reasons why:

- An average of more than one in every hundred homes suffers serious damage each year, mostly caused by fire and weather events.

- Earthquakes have hit 39 states since 1900 and caused damage in all 50 states.

- Almost one-half of all people in the second half of their working lives will suffer a disability lasting more than 90 days before reaching retirement age.

- Most people who reach retirement age will need some level of long-term care in their later lives.

- More than two million homes are burglarized every year, and more than a million cars are stolen.

- The cost of medical care is rising considerably faster than the rate of inflation. Thousands of people die every year because they don't have insurance coverage.

CAN I CUT MY INSURANCE COSTS?

In a word, "Yes."

There are lots of ways to reduce your outlay on insurance premiums. I've already mentioned the use of deductibles, where you agree to pay the first chunk of money on your policy.

This amount may range from a couple of hundred dollars on an auto policy to several thousand on a medical policy. Either way, you will make significant savings. You can also save by taking steps to improve your insurability, for instance, installing security systems at home, improving your general health (using some of the tips in this book), and demonstrating that you are a safe driver.

In addition, you might increase your savings by buying two or more of your policies from the same company and, of course, by shopping around. It's amazing just how much of a difference two insurers will charge for, more or less, the same risks.

The most important step you can take to realize these savings is to discuss your needs with an expert who will help you develop a comprehensive insurance program that works for you and your budget and ensures you're getting every possible discount.

ABOUT THE AUTHORS

Greg grew up in beautiful Lake Chelan, WA, and has always been very active in sports and all outdoor activities throughout his life. In 2001, he attended Eastern Washington University, competing in track as a decathlete and graduating after four years with a BA in Business/Human Resource Management. He then moved to the Tri-Cities in 2006, where he truly enjoys the weather and the outdoor activities of camping, hunting, fishing, golf, etc. He married his amazing wife Danielle in 2009 and created two incredible children, Evan and Emmerson.

Greg Boyd originally started in the insurance realm in 2007 at Country Financial, where he was licensed to write auto, home, business, and life insurance. In 2009, he was hired by an independent insurance agency. For the next 11 years he helped grow that agency and became a leader within. In 2021, Jason Graybeal purchased the agency, and Greg became the integrator/operations manager. As he puts it: "We're on a next-level path, and I couldn't be happier."

Jason Graybeal is the president and founder of Graybeal Group, Inc., a $5 million-plus insurance agency specializing in Agricultural, Commercial and Personal insurance.

From humble beginnings and starting from scratch—twice—Jason has grown and leads a dynamic team of 22 employees.

His mission is to provide high-performing individuals the opportunity and tools to grow and prosper in rural America while protecting and serving customers in the same market.

His specialty is the acquisition of similar companies and incorporating them into his culture and team.

As the host of the *No Bull Business and Brews* podcast, Jason and his team bring business, sales, and life experience to provide value to entrepreneurs and business owners everywhere.

For more information on hiring Jason as a business coach, please visit:

JasonGraybeal.com.

LEGAL DISCLAIMER

All material in this book is provided for information and educational purposes and should not be construed as medical diagnosis or advice or as instruction on security and safety procedures. It is not intended as a substitute for professional advice, which you should always seek regarding safety and health, especially where opinions differ. While we have sought to ensure the information in this book is accurate, the publisher does not accept responsibility for decisions you make as a result of that information, or for any errors and omissions.

Made in the USA
Monee, IL
11 February 2022